365 TV-free Activities for Kids

Di Hodges

HINKLER BOOKS

Published in 2002 by Hinkler Book Pty Ltd
17–23 Redwood Drive
Dingley VIC 3172 Australia
www.hinklerbooks.com

Reprinted 2003
© Hinkler Books Pty Ltd 2002

Written by: Di Hodges
Edited by: Heather Hammonds

ISBN 1 8651 5723 6

This publication is an interactive educational book designed to teach and entertain children.
Some activities will require the use of materials/tools that could cause injury, including
serious injury if swallowed or used. The Publisher, the Editor, or their respective employees or
agents shall not accept responsibility for injury or damage occasioned to any person as a
result from participation in any activity in this book, whether or not such injury, loss or
damage is in any way due to any negligent act or omission, breach of duty or default on the
part of the Publisher, the Editor, or their respective employees or agents.

Printed & bound in Australia.

CONTENTS

FOREWORD

Like many parents, you probably consider that your children spend far too much time watching television or playing on the computer. Recent research has shown that these are the most popular recreational activities for children outside school hours. This has contributed to major concerns in our community regarding the high levels of obesity in our children, which are directly related to sitting down in front of the television or computer, rather than kicking a ball around or being involved in other active play.

While we all know that the television or computer can be great learning tools, countless studies have shown that children learn best from 'doing'. The second-hand experiences they gain from watching the TV or playing on the computer will never replace what children learn through their play and through 'hands-on' experience.

This book is designed to help you get your children involved in a host of exciting activities. Activities to enhance their creativity, increase their knowledge of the world around them, develop their coordination, boost their self-confidence and to provide them with lots of good old-fashioned fun!

While some of the activities require adult participation, others only need a parent's help to get the children started. Safety is of the utmost importance though, and activities using objects such as scissors or knives should be closely supervised.

Turn off the TV or computer and spend some quality time with your children working on the activities in this book. This will help them develop their imaginations and improve their communication skills and stand them in good stead in the years ahead.

*

Di Hodges has been an early childhood teacher for over twenty years. She has taught in a variety of settings, including pre-schools, prep classes and years 1 and 2. She has also spent many years helping geographically isolated parents teach their pre-schoolers at home through Distance Education facilities.

Di has a Diploma of Teaching for Early Childhood and Primary, and a Bachelor of Education. She is currently an Education Advisor (Pre-school) with Education Queensland.

HOW TO USE THIS BOOK

This book is full of ideas that you can enjoy trying with your 5 to 8-year-old children. Each page contains a short list of materials you will need to collect before you begin the activity. More often than not these are everyday household items you will already have. Save junk, as many activities in this book use recycled household junk. Other materials may need to be purchased from newsagents, craft shops or your local discount store.

This book contains two indexes—a subject index at the front of the book and an alphabetical activity index at the back. The book is divided into ten categories:

**Indoor Activities
Let's Create
Food Fun
Word Play
Number Games
Games to Play
Outdoor Activities
Exploring the Environment
Sports Skills
Special Occasions**

The activities in each category of the book have been divided into age groups from 5 to 8-year-olds and sorted alphabetically. There will be something that is exactly right for your child. The suggested age on each activity is a guide only—remember that all children are different and you'll soon know if an activity is too easy or too difficult for your child.

Start with easy activities, give lots of praise and then move on to harder activities.

This book will help you find those areas of learning that your child needs extra time and help with. Don't forget that to succeed at school and in life, our children need a healthy self-image and parents can foster this with lots of praise, encouragement, time and love. Have fun together!

GUIDE TO SYMBOLS

These simple symbols give a quick visual reference to the basic elements present in each activity.

 Outdoor activity: This symbol indicates an outdoor activity.

 Indoor activity: This symbol indicates an indoor activity. **Note:** If both symbols are present, the activity can be enjoyed both outdoors and indoors.

 Adult participation: This activity requires some degree of adult supervision. Read the 'What To Do' closely, to see the degree of monitoring required. This symbol can also indicate that participation with an adult is important for learning or sharing.

 Pencils, paints and paper: This activity requires basic drawing or painting tools. It can be as simple as a pencil and paper for keeping score in a game, or art materials for decorating etc.

 Tools required: This activity requires tools of some type. This could be anything from a simple bowl and vegetable peeler, to balloons and craft materials. Most activities have been designed to use basic everyday items found in the home, such as cereal boxes. Some activities may require items to be purchased, but they should be inexpensive or alternatives can be used. Read the 'What You Need' for specific items. Adult supervision is required.

Learning and imagination: Just about all of the activities in this book encourage imaginative play. There are activities that require some adult participation and may contain important learning skills, designed for fun. If the activity is simply a game to occupy a bored child, this symbol will not be present.

INDOOR
ACTIVITIES

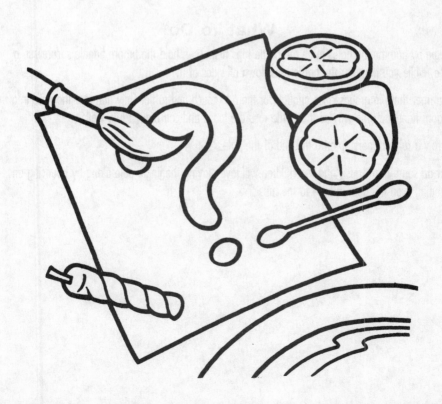

JINGLE POLES

Many folk bands use these simple poles to make music.
They are a great instrument to play and keep the beat with.

What You Need

- Broom handle • Hammer • Nails
- Beer bottle tops • Vice • Rubber doorstop

What To Do

Begin by hammering holes in all the bottle tops first. Then hold the broom handle securely in a vice, while you hammer the bottle tops down all sides of it.

Hammer them in groups close enough for them to touch and rattle. Only hammer the nails into the broom handle a little way so the bottle tops are loose and can really rattle well.

Screw a rubber doorstop onto the end of the pole.

Put on some bush music and the children will love playing the jingle pole along by bouncing and banging it on the floor in time to the music.

NAILING FUN

An activity that encourages the development of excellent hand-eye coordination.

What You Need

- Small nails • Small tack hammer
- Piece of pine board about 25 cm (9 ³/₄ in) square
- Threading material

What To Do

If you are buying a piece of pine for this activity the above size is ideal, but really any shape will be fine as long as it is large enough to work on. Timber furniture makers are always happy to let you have their pine off-cuts. Pine is ideal for hammering with young children because it is a soft timber.

Mark dots about 2 cm (³/₄ in) apart around the outside of the board and your children can hammer a nail part of the way into each dot. Then give them a selection of wool, string, elastic, raffia or even coloured wire to wind from nail to nail, to make interesting patterns and shapes.

Another time you might like to mark the dots in the shape of a circle or perhaps a star to make a different pattern for your children to try.

PUPPET THEATRE

*Make a simple puppet theatre and your children will love putting on their own
'productions' with the home-made puppets they have been making.*

What You Need

- Acrylic or fabric paints • Calico or other cheap white fabric
- Your sewing machine • Stretch wire • Hooks

What To Do

To calculate the width of the puppet theatre, measure the width of your children's bedroom doorway and double it. For the height, have your children kneel in the doorway. Measure just above their heads so they'll be hidden and add enough for a hem at the top and bottom of the theatre.

Sew up the curtain and thread the stretch wire through the top. Then attach the curtain and wire to a hook on either side of your children's bedroom doorway.

I am sure they will want to decorate the puppet theatre with acrylic paints or fabric paints but take it down again and do it outside.

When it's dry, hang it up and 'on with the show'. When not in use, roll it up and store it in the wardrobe.

SOFT DRINK BOTTLE MUSIC

Pre-schools and kindergartens have long been the best recyclers of junk. Plastic soft drink bottles have many uses—for storage, for scoops in the sand pit and even for musical instruments. Save some and make a wind ensemble with your children.

What You Need
- Food colouring • Water
- Plastic soft drink bottles

What To Do

Making music out of a plastic soft drink bottle is incredibly simple. Just hold it up to your lips and gently blow across the top of the empty bottle. You can vary the pitch by putting different amounts of coloured water into some of the bottles and make a whole range of sounds. Soft drink bottle music will provide your children with lots of cheap musical fun.

ANIMAL, VEGETABLE OR MINERAL

This is a good guessing game to play with your children and will keep them amused on rainy days and on long car trips.

What You Need

- Players

What To Do

Think of an object or person that will be 'it'. The categories in this game are Animal (people, animals, insects, etc.), Vegetable (plants) and Mineral (iron, inanimate objects).

Your children can then ask twenty questions to try and determine what 'it' is. Except for the first question, which traditionally asks if it is 'Animal, Vegetable or Mineral', all the other questions are just answered with a 'Yes' or a 'No'.

The person being asked the questions must keep track of the number of questions they are asked. If there is more than one person asking the questions, the first person to guess the answer on or before the twentieth question has the next turn.

Hint!

If you find your children are getting 'bogged down' by the questions, give them some clues until they begin to understand the game!

COMB SYNTHESISER

6+

*Show your children how to make music with nothing more than
a comb, some tissue paper and their lips!*

What You Need

• Comb • Tissue paper

What To Do

Tell your children you are going to make a music synthesiser that does not need electricity. Wrap a few layers of tissue paper around a comb and hold it up to your lips and hum. See if your children can recognise the tune.

Now give your children a turn. Ask them if it tickles their lips when they hum. Make several comb synthesisers and make a fun (and noisy) comb band!

PING PONG BLOW

This game was a favourite with my sister and I when we were younger. Like many families, we had a table-tennis table set up under the house and we both loved playing it. But we also loved this simple game of blowing the table tennis ball.

What You Need

- A ping pong ball
- A large flat surface—a table is ideal

What To Do

This game is incredibly simple and yet it will keep children occupied for hours. One child is at one end of a table and another child at the opposite end. They take it in turns to blow the ball to the opposite end (or side of the table for younger players without so much puff).

If you can blow your ball past your opponent, you score a point. You cannot touch the ball with your hands—you must only blow to keep it from going over the end of the table.

Lots of simple fun and a great inside game on wet, boring days.

PULSE BEAT

Show your children a simple way of finding out how fast their heart is beating with this easy experiment.

What You Need

- Playdough or plasticine • Toothpicks

What To Do

Form a small ball of playdough and stick a toothpick into it. Have your children hold out their arm straight and keep it totally still. Place the ball of playdough on their wrist where the pulse is (you may need to move it around to find the strongest beat). Watch what happens to the toothpick.

Have your children run around for a little while or jump up and down a few times, and let them observe their pulse after exercise. Put the playdough ball on your own arm and they can see your pulse too.

Explain to your children that they saw the toothpick move because they are seeing the blood being pumped around their body by their heart. Doctors measure pulse rates to find out if a person's heart is beating at a normal rate.

Your children might enjoy counting the pulse rates of various members of the family to see who has the fastest heartbeat.

6+

SECRET MESSAGES

*Children love intrigue and mystery. Writing secret messages to their best friend
(so brothers and sisters can't read them) will quickly become a favourite activity.*

What You Need

- Paper • Candles • Cotton buds
- Watercolour paint • Lemon juice

What To Do

There are two ways to write secret messages. The simplest way is to write on a piece of white paper with a candle. When your children's friends want to read the message, they paint over the paper with a wash of watercolour paint.

The other method is to write the message with lemon juice using a cotton bud. When it's dry, dip the paper in water and the message can be read.

COIN SPINNING

I am indebted to my mother-in-law for this activity. She and her brothers and sisters loved playing this when they were children.

What You Need

• Coins • Pins

What To Do

Carefully hold a coin between two pins that are exactly opposite each other. Then gently blow on the coin to make it spin. Ask your children to see who can make their coin spin the fastest. When they have mastered the trick, see if they can do it with different sized coins.

This activity needs close adult supervision because of the use of sharp pins. Make sure that the pins are put away safely when the activity is over and keep them out of the reach of younger children.

COLLECTIONS

*Being a collector will help your children develop organisational
skills that will be very useful later in life.*

What You Need

- Try to encourage your children to collect more unusual items than football or basketball cards.
- Some things your child might like to collect: Autographs, Shells, Rubbers, Badges, Keys, Drink coasters, Beads, Labels, Stamps, Bookmarks, Marbles, Stickers, Bottle tops, Match boxes, Matchbox cars, Crystals, Corals, Bus or train tickets, Buttons, Pencils, Dolls, Cards (greeting), Postcards, Dolls clothes, Coins, Rocks, Tazos.

What To Do

The most difficult part of any collection is finding the best way to store it.

Photo albums are great for storing items like bus tickets, postcards, labels and cards. Badges can be pinned on bedroom curtains and a cork notice board in your children's room can display lots of items also. Large clear bowls (fish bowls or tanks are ideal) can hold other collections.

Encourage your children to be selective collectors. Suggest that they keep doubles for swapping with their friends or other collectors.

If you have a computer at home and are linked into the Internet, this is a great way to meet up with other collectors for swaps.

FINGERPRINTS

Explain to your children that everyone has different fingerprints.
Then show them how to fingerprint the whole family!

What You Need

- Small soft paintbrush • Stamp pad
- Cornflour • Magnifying glass

What To Do

Help your children fingerprint family members by placing each person's index finger on the stamp pad and rolling it backwards and forwards. Then place the finger on a piece of paper and again roll it backwards and forwards. Write the person's name beside each fingerprint.

Now your children can play the detective and look for fingerprints in the house, and see if they can identify them. When they find one, show them how to lightly dust it with cornflour using the little paintbrush. Then they carefully blow away the excess cornflour and they'll be able to clearly see the fingerprint. They may need to use a magnifying glass to identify the print. Sherlock Holmes!

Now you'll be able to find out who's been raiding the fridge and the biscuit jar!

NURSING HOME VISITS

Encourage community care in your children by taking them to visit nursing home residents who don't have regular visitors.

What You Need

- Time

What To Do

One of my grandmothers died recently, aged 97. For the last four years of her life she lived in a nursing home and we all visited as much as we could. It was always very sad, however, to see how many of the elderly residents didn't receive regular visitors. They always especially loved seeing any children who visited the nursing home.

Ring a nursing home close to where you live and ask if there are any residents who would like a regular visit from your family. Children can learn so much from the wisdom of older people and learn about caring for others. Even learning to cope with grief when they lose an older friend or relative is something children need to experience.

Doing things to help others enriches our own lives so much.

PLAITING

Many children have never learnt to master this interesting skill. Learning to plait will help develop your children's manual dexterity and provide lots of fun.

What You Need

- Lengths of heavy wool, thin rope or twine, or long strands of interesting fabric

What To Do

Tie three equal lengths of the plaiting material together. When your children are learning to plait, it's a good idea to use three different colours. This will make it easier for them. Attach the plaiting material to the back of a chair or a door knob and separate the strands so there is a left, a centre and a right strand.

The left hand strand goes over the centre one and then the right hand stand goes over the new centre one, the original left strand and so on. Continue plaiting, left to the centre, right to the centre. Tie off when the plait is finished.

If your children are really 'into' this activity, they could plait lots of lengths of fabrics (a great way to empty the rag box) and later you can help them sew them together to make an old-fashioned rag mat, to put beside their bed or use as a bath mat.

HOME-MADE PIANO

This is a great idea for older children to try, or an adult could make it for their younger children.

What You Need

- Bolts, washers and wing nuts • Drill • Off-cuts of pine
- Ice-cream sticks • Plastic flower pots • Saw • Vice

What To Do

This idea is based on a thumb piano which originally came from Africa. Begin with two pieces of pine about 15 cm (6 in) long and 4 cm (1.5 in) wide. Drill through both pieces of wood at both ends and then bolt together the two pieces of wood with a long bolt.

Push the ice-cream sticks into the space between the pieces of wood. Begin with only a small piece of ice-cream stick poking out and work up to a long piece so the pieces resemble the short to long keys on a piano. The short sticks will make the high notes and the long sticks will make the low notes. Tighten up the wing nuts when all the ice-cream sticks are in place.

Put the piano on a hard, flat surface. Hold it down firmly with one hand and you will be able to pick out simple tunes with the other hand. If you want more resonance, place the piano on two plastic flowerpots which have holes cut out of each side and the notes will echo through the holes.

The children will love their simple home-made piano. Perhaps older children could use their local library to research the origins of this strange instrument.

A DAY IN THE LIFE OF YOUR FAMILY VIDEO

If you don't own or can't borrow one, hire a video camera for a day and capture some shots of your family to look at in the future.

What You Need

- A family day together • A video camera

What To Do

Video cameras are very user-friendly today and, like most technology, our kids are better with them than us. Your older children will love making a video of a day in the life of your family.

Begin with normal family shots of everyone having breakfast and so on. Perhaps you could go for a picnic or somewhere special so the day is really different. Videoing special occasions such as a birthday is always a good idea too.

Your children may prefer to simply video everyone doing their normal weekend activities such as gardening, cleaning the car, washing the dog, having a roast for Saturday night dinner or a barbecue with friends. Make sure your children are in the video too; sometimes the person holding the camera gets left out!

In years to come, your family videos will provide lots of laughs and great opportunities for reminiscing.

KNOTTING—A BOWLINE

Older children enjoy the challenge of learning how to make new knots.

What You Need

- Rope

What To Do

A bowline forms a loop which will not slip but is still easy to untie. Decide how large the loop will be and measure off that much rope. In the remaining rope make a small loop and then bring the end of the large loop through the small loop and around the back. Continue by passing the end of the rope back down through the small loop and pull tight.

Hint!

Always check knots children have made before they use them for any purpose.

KNOTTING—
A CLOVE HITCH

Older children will enjoy learning how to make different knots.
Here is another knot for them to try.

What You Need
- Rope

What To Do

A clove hitch is a useful knot to use for securing a rope to a railing or a similar object.

Put the end of the rope over the railing and then back around, crossing over its own hanging part. Continue by passing the end over the railing again, making a loop.

Then pass the end right around the railing. Bring the end back through the loop that has formed and pull tight.

Hint!

Always check knots children have made before they use them for any purpose.

KNOTTING— A FISHERMAN'S KNOT

Older children love learning how to tie knots for various purposes.
A fisherman's knot is a very handy knot for them to learn.

What You Need

- Two pieces of rope

What To Do

This knot is great for joining together two pieces of rope of similar size. It makes a very strong knot.

Put the two ends of the rope together with about a 0.5 m (1 ½ ft) overlap. Take the end of the first rope over and under the second rope and under itself to form a loop. Next push the end of this rope through the loop to make an overhand knot in the end of the first rope, around the second rope.

Repeat the process with the second rope so you now have two loose knots—one in each rope. Pull them tight and the two knots will slide together and form a very secure join.

Hint!

Always check knots children have made before they use them for any purpose.

KNOTTING—A REEF KNOT

Grandpa may laugh and say that this is not the way he used to tie reef knots, but I have found this is a simple method to teach children how to tie them.

What You Need

- Two pieces of rope

What To Do

This knot makes a very secure way to join two ropes together.

Form a loop in the first rope. Then bring the end of the second rope up through this loop. Next, take the end of the second rope over the standing part of the first. Pass the end of the second rope completely behind the loop made in the first rope, making a circle around it. Then take the end of the second rope back over the end of the first rope. Finally thread the end of the second rope down through the loop alongside its own standing part and pull tight.

Hint!

Always check knots children have made before they use them for any purpose.

LET'S
CREATE

APPLE PRINT BOOK PAPER

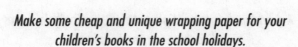

*Make some cheap and unique wrapping paper for your
children's books in the school holidays.*

What You Need

- Apples • Vegetable knife
- Poster paint (available from chain stores or craft shops)
- Plate • Butcher's paper or a roll of newsprint
- Newspaper

What To Do

Go to your local newspaper office and for a small sum you can buy the end of a roll of newsprint paper. This will last the children for years and is ideal for drawing, painting and printing.

Children's school books look better covered and last longer too. If you cover them all in the same paper, littlies can recognise them fast.

Cover an outdoor table with some newspaper and help them cut some apples in half. Pat the cut side of the apple dry. Then dip the apple in a thin layer of paint and let the children print all over the paper. Use a few different colours if they wish—red, yellow or green. When the paper is dry they will love helping you cover their school books. Slip on a plastic cover or cover the books with clear adhesive plastic to make them even stronger.

Hint!

Vegetables such as mushrooms, carrots, onions and potatoes are great for printing, too.

ART IN THE DARK

*A good family activity to play at night, especially in storms
when there is a power failure!*

What You Need

- Paper • Pencils

What To Do

Hand everyone a pencil and paper and make sure they can draw comfortably. Turn out all the lights.

First, everyone writes their name at the top of the paper. Then tell them what to draw—perhaps a cow, your house or Mum, or anything else you can think of. When everyone is finished, turn the lights back on and have a laugh at the results.

Move over, Picasso!

BEACH ART

Collect lots of beach treasures with the children to enable them to enjoy creating some beach art at home.

What You Need

- Bits and pieces from the beach such as seaweed, sponges, shells, small stones, little pieces of driftwood, beach grass and so on
- Strong PVA glue • Cardboard

What To Do

Take some buckets or other containers to the beach and, before you go home, go for a walk with the children to gather lots of treasures. Save them for a rainy day or a day when everyone is tired or bored. Spread them out on a table and provide some PVA glue in small dishes or plastic containers, with brushes and a variety of cardboard.

This messy activity is ideal to do on a table out-of-doors and any left over bits and pieces can simply be hosed or swept into the garden.

You will be amazed at the wonderful creations your children will make, and they will be very special mementos of a day or holiday at the beach for your children.

DINOSAUR PUPPETS

Kids are absolutely fascinated by dinosaurs. Research them together and help your children make a dinosaur puppet stage and dinosaur puppets.

What You Need

• Felt pens • Glue • Scissors • Stiff cardboard

What To Do

Fold a large piece of cardboard at both ends so it can stand on its own. Your children can use their imagination to decorate it with dinosaur 'scenery'—rocks, mountains, perhaps a volcano, water, etc. Look in books about dinosaurs together for ideas.

Then help your children to draw or trace pictures of dinosaurs onto more cardboard and carefully cut them out. Tape stiff cardboard tabs about 10 cm long and 3 cm wide onto the dinosaurs, to hold them in place. Cut slits in the puppet theatre where your children want the dinosaurs to move.

Place the puppet theatre on the edge of a table. Your children stand or sit behind the theatre and move the dinosaur puppets as they tell the story. Help them work out a little play to perform for the rest of the family, or for their class at school.

EGG SHELL PICTURES

Help your children make interesting textured pictures from egg shells. They could also use them to decorate unique cards for birthdays and other special occasions.

What You Need

- Dyed egg shells • Plastic containers for storage
- Strong glue • Cardboard

What To Do

Save all the egg shells from cooking or from boiled eggs. Wash them well and dry in the sun before storing. When you have quite a lot you can dye them in batches, using strong solutions of food dye. Again, dry them well in the sun after dyeing. Your children will enjoy helping you with the dyeing but don't forget to wear rubber or plastic gloves, or your hands will look like the Incredible Hulk's!

Your children can then crush the egg shells with a roller or with a meat mallet. It is easiest to do this on a kitchen board covered with a tea towel. When they have finished, pick up the tea towel and pour the pieces carefully into a container for each colour.

Now your children can be creative with all the lovely dyed egg shells. They can draw pictures onto the cardboard first, before painting them with glue and covering them with egg shells. Or they can place the egg shells directly onto the glued cardboard in more abstract patterns.

5+

EYE DROPPER PAINTING

This activity teaches your children how to mix the three basic colours to form new ones.

What You Need

- Plastic eye droppers (cheap to buy or save the ones that come with children's medicines)
  - Red, yellow or blue powder paint, or food colouring mixed with water

---

What To Do

A good activity to do on a table or tarpaulin outside. If it's going to be an inside activity, spread lots of newspapers on your table.

Provide three eye droppers and three jars or paint pots with the colours red, yellow and blue. Provide plenty of paper and let your children experiment with making new colours.

Encourage your children not to make the paper too wet with paint or it tears when hung up. Wet paintings can be hung on a clothes drier to dry, or even the clothes line.

Sometimes it is fun to wet the paper first with plain water and see what happens when the colours are squirted on. Use small bottles of food colouring to do this.

FINGERPRINT CRITTERS

5+

*Your children can use their imaginations to create
interesting 'critters' from their fingerprints.*

What You Need

- Pens or coloured pencils
- Stamp pad or coloured felt pens
- Paper

What To Do

Show your children how to make fingerprints by pressing their index finger in the stamp pad, rolling it from side to side. Then carefully place it on the paper and again roll it from side to side to produce a clear print.

If you don't have a stamp pad, they can colour their index finger with a non-permanent felt pen and then make a print (have a cloth nearby to wipe fingers on—you don't want fingerprints all over the walls).

Then your children can add details to turn their fingerprints into whatever they like such as birds, flowers, people, bugs, monsters or anything else they can think of. Think of some of your own too!

FLYING HELICOPTERS

*Make this fun flying object together. Launch it from
the verandah and see how far it can fly.*

What You Need

- An old postcard or a small piece of cardboard
- Scissors • Paper clip

What To Do

Help your children to measure and cut a 3 cm (1 ¼ in) wide strip off the postcard. In this strip, make two slits at two-thirds of the length of the card.

Hold a corner in each hand and twist, and then bring the ends together and secure with a paper clip.

The kids will love dropping the helicopter from up high and watching it as it whirls around.

LEAF SPLATTER PICTURES

This is a great outdoor activity, but make sure the kids are wearing old clothes or put on an old shirt of Dad's as an art smock.

What You Need

- Leaves, flowers, seedpods • Paper
- Acrylic paint (available from toy stores, craft shops)
- A nailbrush • Blu-Tac • Masking tape
- Some fine wire stapled to an old picture frame
- Cereal box with one side cut out

What To Do

Place a sheet of paper inside the box, held down with a little Blu-Tac so it doesn't slip.

Place the flowers and leaves on the paper. Then put the wire screen over the box and dip the nailbrush into the paint. As the children rub the brush over the screen the paint will splatter and mark the paper, except where the leaves and flowers are. When you carefully remove the leaves they will have very interesting splatter paintings.

It is also interesting for the children to use different coloured paints and see the colours mix and make new colours—perhaps yellow and blue to form green.

Hint!

The screen will need to be hosed from time to time as it will fill with paint.

ICE-CREAM STICK CREATIONS

Collect ice-cream sticks or buy them cheaply from craft or junk stores and your kids will love creating all sorts of exciting things from them.

What You Need

- Newspaper • Ice-cream sticks
- Paint • Strong PVA or craft glue

What To Do

Spread some newspaper on a table so the glue won't stick and ask your children to work out what they would like to make. They could make something they could use, like a small box, by laying sticks in a square shape and gradually building it up. Or they could simply create something like a plane or an animal.

Most children are far more inventive than us 'oldies' and they will have lots of fun making wonderful creations. Just remind them that the glue does dry clear if it looks messy and that PVA and craft glue will need some time to dry. When the creation is dry they will enjoy painting it.

PAINTED ROCKS

*Paperweights are useful for everyone. Help your children
make some for gifts, or for their own use.*

What You Need

- Small rocks of a suitable size • Small brushes
- House or acrylic paints

What To Do

Next time you have a family picnic at the beach or near a creek or river, see if you can find some nice smooth rocks that would be suitable for paperweights. Take some home and keep them for a rainy day, or for when the children are bored and looking for something different to do.

Cover an outdoor table with newspaper or an old cloth and find a selection of small brushes. You will need to use acrylic or house paints for this project. You can buy small sample tins of some brands of acrylic paints from hardware stores or paint shops and they are ideal for activities like these. Otherwise, visit a craft store to buy some acrylic craft paints.

The children will have great fun painting and decorating their rocks and, when they are dry, they can give them to friends and family for gifts.

Hint!

Acrylic paint is often difficult to wash out of clothes. Avoid this problem by giving the children old adult sized shirt or T-shirts to wear over their clothes. If they do get some on their clothes, soak in warm water before washing and do not spray with a pre-wash spray as this often sets the paint.

PLASTICINE PLAY

A different medium for creating models, plasticine is cheap to buy, and lots of fun.

What You Need

- Plasticine—available from newsagents, school suppliers and toy shops

What To Do

While playdough is cheap to make at home, buying plasticine will give your children a different medium for modelling. Because it is firmer than playdough, it keeps its style better and is a great way to strengthen finger and hand muscles.

Plasticine usually comes in a variety of colours, which adds another interesting dimension to creating. Sit down with your children and shown them how to model people, animals and other shapes. They might like to create a whole plasticine environment—a dinosaur landscape or perhaps a farm.

For added interest, pipe-cleaners, matches, ice-cream sticks, beads and other things can be used with the plasticine.

PLAYDOUGH PRINT PAPER

5+

Make some interesting wrapping paper with the children using playdough.

What You Need

- Collection of objects that have an interesting textured surface
- Kitchen sponges • Playdough • Plastic, baking or polystyrene trays
- Poster or acrylic paints • Large sheets of butcher's paper or similar

What To Do

Go for a walk around the garden and in the house with the children, and collect objects that have an interesting textured surface such as rocks, bark, leaves, sticks, toys, Lego blocks, kitchen utensils and so on.

Roll some playdough into balls and press them onto the surface of the objects to make imprints of the texture.

Then pour a little of each coloured paint onto the kitchen sponges. Place the sponges in a tray to use as a stamp pad and the children can print with the playdough balls.

The result will be very interesting patterns on the paper and it will look great as wrapping paper for special occasion gifts.

Hint!

If you sprinkle glitter on red and green paint while it is still wet, the paper will look very Christmassy!

POTATO MEN

Potatoes have such interesting shapes and they make wonderful 'men'! Show your children how they can do this with a few bits and pieces and lots of imagination.

What You Need

- Large potatoes • Small scrubbing brush
- Playdough or plasticine • Toothpicks
- Bits and pieces to decorate with—lace, felt, fabric scraps, coloured paper, ribbons and so on

What To Do

Give your children a large bowl of warm water and they can begin by scrubbing all the dirt off their potatoes. Next they dry them with a tea towel. Now they are ready to begin making Potato Men.

Help your children use the toothpicks (some may have to be shortened) to hold the playdough or plasticine in place for the facial features—eyes, nose, mouth and ears.

Now they can use the fabric, paper and so on to make bow tie, hats and other clothes. Cotton wool dyed black or brown can be used as hair or perhaps a moustache. Lady Potato People might like a ribbon or bow in their hair. Help the children make a whole Potato Family.

When they've finished the project they can scrub fresh potatoes for a yummy snack. Show them how to rub the skins with olive oil. Bake in a fairly hot oven. When they are crispy on the outside and soft in the middle, take them out. Cut off the tops, scoop out some of the middle and mix with grated cheese and ham. Pop them back in the oven for a few minutes to reheat.

A very 'more-ish' snack, or a simple and easy tea that your children will love.

POTATO PRINTS

Children of all ages love printing, so here is another way they can make their own colourful and creative wrapping paper.

What You Need

- Potatoes • Small, sharp kitchen knife • Thin felt pen
- Lots of newspaper • Paint made from food colouring and wall paper paste, or commercial paint • Kitchen sponges
- Paper or card • Styrofoam trays

What To Do

Cut the potatoes in half and suggest to your children that they draw a simple design with the thin felt pen on the potato halves. Next, cut carefully around the shapes for them. Older children may be able to do this for themselves, with supervision.

Put the kitchen sponges on the Styrofoam trays and pour a little paint on each—a different colour on each one.

Put plenty of newspaper on a flat working surface and show them how to print by pushing down firmly on the sponge and then printing on their paper. If you have some cardboard, your children might like to print some cards. Keep them for use in the future. The printed paper makes excellent wrapping paper and everyone will be impressed by the children's creativity.

TREASURE CHESTS

5+

Children love having special little boxes in which to store treasured possessions.
Show your children how simply they can be made out of household junk.

What You Need

- Empty tetra-pak juice containers
- A ruler and a pen • Craft knife or scissors
- Sticky tape • Paint and other materials for decoration

What To Do

Decide with the children how large they want their special box to be. Measure the distance from the bottom of the juice container and draw a cutting line with the ruler and pen. Cut along the two sides of the pack and the front at this point, but not the back.

Next, form the lid from the remaining long piece at the back of the box. Measure the depth and width of the box, add them together (older children can do this—it's great maths practice) and mark this on the lid flap. Cut carefully and then bend the lid over in the appropriate places.

Your children will enjoy decorating their own special box. They can begin by painting it—household paints work well, or acrylic paints. Then decorate the boxes with glitter, sequins, bits of ribbon, lace or fabric off-cuts, pretty flowers or leaves from the garden, pictures cut from greeting cards or magazines, or their own art work.

To keep the box closed, use some adhesive velcro (available from sewing shops) or a button on a loop at the front.

WET CHALK DRAWINGS

*Soak sticks of coloured chalk in water to provide
a different drawing medium for your children.*

What You Need

- Water • Coloured chalk sticks
- Paper (if you want to spend a little money,
buy some black paper—the effect is terrific)

What To Do

Your children can help you soak the chalk sticks in water for about ten minutes. Warn them not to press too hard as they draw because the chalk can break easily.

Drawing with wet chalk on black paper looks especially effective, but it's just as interesting on white.

Happy drawing!

BAKED BEADS

*Help your children make colourful necklaces for themselves
or original gifts for others with this simple recipe.*

What You Need

- Acrylic paints • Brushes • 4 cups of plain flour
- 1 cup of salt • 1½ cups of cold water • Fishing line

What To Do

Mix the flour and salt together and then add the water. Knead for at least ten minutes on a floured board (let your children help with the measuring and kneading). Measuring is a great maths activity and kneading is good for small muscle development. Knead until the craft dough is pliable and will not fall to bits.

Help your children mould the dough into interesting bead shapes. Use a nail, skewer or kebab stick to make a hole through the centre of each bead.

Bake the beads in a slow oven for 2–3 hours until they are hard and completely dry.

Once the beads have cooled, your children can paint them in bright colours. Thread with fishing line when the paint is totally dry.

BATIK FOR KIDS

Conventional batik needs hot wax and this is dangerous with young children.
Use this safe batik to make interesting fabric designs.

What You Need

- White cotton fabric (sheeting material is fine) or T-shirts
- Brushes • Water • Flour • Old detergent container
- Cold water dyes (available from chemists and supermarkets)

What To Do

Together, make up a paste from flour and water and pour it into an old detergent bottle. Your children can squeeze paste onto the T-shirt or fabric in whatever design they like. When the paste is dry, make up the cold water dyes, provide the brushes and they can paint the glue-free areas.

When the garment or fabric is dry they will have their own fabric art work. You could make the fabric into some great big comfy cushions on which to read books in their bedroom.

BEAUTIFUL FLOWER PICTURES

Preserve the beauty of spring flowers with your children.

What You Need

- A selection of small spring flowers • A tea towel
- Grease proof paper • A cool iron
- Hole punch • Thin coloured satin ribbon

What To Do

Go for a walk in your garden with your children and gather a selection of small, dainty spring flowers and leaves.

Spread them out on a table outdoors (so the remaining flowers and leaves can simply be swept or hosed into the garden) and select flowers that go together well in pictures.

Cut out pieces of the grease proof paper and lay the selected flowers and leaves on one piece and cover with another. Put the tea towel over the top and iron carefully with a cool iron. The wax in the paper will melt the paper together sealing in the flowers and leaves.

Help the children cut around their pretty pictures, punch a hole at the top of each picture and thread some ribbon through for hanging.

A lovely bedroom decoration and a way to keep spring in your home all year.

CLAY WIND CHIMES

6+

Nothing sounds as enchanting as simple wind chimes tinkling in the breeze.

What You Need

- Clay • Boards or a plastic sheet or tablecloth to work on
- Implements to print with—cutlery, Lego, sticks from the garden, etc • A friendly potter who will fire the chimes

What To Do

Before clay can be fired it needs to be wedged, which helps give the clay even consistency and removes any air bubbles that could pop in the kiln and make the clay piece explode. Children can easily be taught how to wedge clay. Show them how to cut their lump of clay in half with a piece of string or fishing line. Then they can bang both pieces together as hard as they can a few times to push out any air in the clay; they really enjoy this. Show how to knead the clay like bread, pushing it backwards and forwards and punching it down hard for a few minutes. By now the clay should have no air bubbles left and will be ready to sculpt, and later to fire.

To make the wind chimes the clay needs to be rolled, or pushed with the fingers. You can show your children how to do this with a rolling pin or by pushing down with your fingers. Next, with an old knife, help them cut out some shapes for the wind chimes; these can be circular, rectangular, or just oblongs or even a mixture of each. To give the wind chimes some texture, press into them the cutlery, Lego or other tools. When the children are satisfied, make a hole in each wind chime with a large darning needle and take them carefully to be fired.

When you get the chimes back, help the children thread fishing line through each one and attach them to some drift wood or an interestingly shaped branch so the chimes can touch each other. Hang the wind chimes where you can hear them tinkle in the breeze and be reminded of your children's creativity.

6+

ENVIRONMENTAL WEAVING

*Show the children how to make a wonderful environmental
weaving to decorate an empty wall at home.*

What You Need

• A large tree branch • Natural items such as feathers, grasses,
leaves, strips of bark, seed pods, corn husks, wheat, etc. • Wool

What To Do

Go for a walk in the park and find a suitable branch with at least two or three small branches
coming out of it to form a triangular shape.

Tie the wool onto the branch and wrap around the other branches to form the warp. Show the
children some loosely woven fabric such as hessian, so they understand about weaving and
the warp and the weft.

Collect lots of natural materials to form an interesting weft. The children will enjoy weaving
the items they find in and out of the warp threads. Coloured wool and strips of fabric could be
used also.

When it is finished the weaving looks great hanging from a wall or hung securely from the ceiling.
Everyone will be very proud of this unique piece of family art.

HOLE-PUNCH PICTURES

6+

A new skill to teach your children that helps develop their fine motor skills.

What You Need

- Felt-pens • Hole puncher • Polystyrene trays (butchers and greengrocers often use these) or thin card • Threading materials

What To Do

After your children have drawn a colourful picture on the card or polystyrene, show them how to punch holes around either the outline of the picture or the border. The holes should be about 3 cm (1 ¼ in) apart.

Your children will then enjoy lacing in and out of the holes. Use a bodkin (blunt ended large needle) threaded with wool or thin embroidery cotton. If you don't want them to use a needle they could lace with plastic lacing (available by the metre from craft shops and haberdasheries) or old shoelaces. They could also use wool or string that has a strengthened end made by dipping it into melted candle wax or a strong solution of laundry starch and allowed to dry.

The pictures can be hung up with another length of the threading material.

JUMPING JACKS

Make some Jumping Jacks with the children and give Dad a big surprise.

What You Need

- Strong paper—typing or photocopy paper is ideal
- Scissors • Glue • A strong, wide rubber band

What To Do

Measure two 10 cm (4 in) squares on the paper and your children can cut them out. Roll each square tightly into a thin cylinder and glue in place so they do not unroll. When the glue has dried, bend each cylinder in the middle and then wrap them together with the rubber band around the middle.

Hold one of the cylinders firmly while you wind the other up as tightly as possible. Carefully place the Jumping Jack inside a box or perhaps a book. Ask someone to open it and watch their face!

LAVENDER SACHETS

Most gardens have a bush of one of the many lovely lavender varieties.
When your lavender is flowering profusely, pick the flowers to
make delightful scented lavender sachets together.

What You Need

- Lavender flowers • Marking pen • Muslin or other thin cloth
- Large bottle • Pinking shears • Narrow lavender ribbon

What To Do

Help your children pick flower heads that are nearly all open and spread them in the sun for a few days to dry. The flowers are easily detached by running your fingers along the stem to strip them off the stalk.

Make the muslin sachets by tracing around a bottle with chalk and then cutting out the circles with pinking shears. Your children can put a few spoonfuls of the lavender flowers in the middle of each muslin circle and then tie securely with the lavender ribbon.

Put some lavender sachets on coat hangers in your wardrobes, in drawers with clothes and in the linen cupboard. The crisp, strong smell helps repel insects.

They also make great gifts.

6+

LEAF PLASTER CASTS

Preserve the interesting textures and shapes of leaves by imprinting them in plaster.

What You Need

- Leaves of all shapes and textures
- Plaster of Paris • Plasticine

What To Do

Go for a walk in the botanical gardens, park or in your own garden and collect a variety of leaves from the ground.

Roll out some plasticine and carefully press some leaves into it using the side of the leaves where the veins are the most prominent. Form a wall of plasticine around the impressions and pour some plaster of Paris into the mould. Leave this to set for a few days, remove the plasticine and the children will have a permanent record of the lovely leaves they collected.

They may enjoy painting their leaf moulds in interesting colours.

54

LEAF RUBBINGS

Here is another way to encourage your children's interest in the trees and plants in their environment. Try making some leaf rubbing pictures together.

What You Need

- Leaves of different shapes and sizes
- Blu-Tac • Thin paper • Crayons

What To Do

Go for a walk together in a park or in your own garden and gather a collection of interesting leaves. Leaves that have interesting shapes and prominent veins make really effective rubbings.

Use a little Blu-Tac to hold the leaves in a place on the table. The rubbings work best if you rub the underside of the leaf where the veins are most prominent. Remove any wrappings from the crayons. Place the paper over a leaf and rub a crayon back and forth across the paper over the leaf. The veins and ridges of the leaf and its outline will appear clearly on the paper.

Use a range of colours and different shaped leaves on each piece of paper. Leaf rubbings make very pretty and unusual wrapping paper. Tuck a few leaves into a ribbon bow around the gift for an even prettier effect.

6+

PAPIER MÂCHÉ BOWLS

*My friend Kerenne, a primary school teacher, makes these
bowls with the children in her class to give to their mums for Christmas.
A useful and colourful gift idea she has shared with us.*

What You Need

- Picnic set bowl or plate • Vaseline • Glue (wallpaper paste is excellent)
- Newspaper and butcher's paper • Acrylic paint

What To Do

Any shaped bowl or plate can be the basic mould for your children's papier mâché creation, but Kerenne prefers to use plastic in case of accidents. Cover the bowl really well with Vaseline before applying the papier mâché so it can lift off well when it is dry.

Apply the newspaper in strips. Dip into the wallpaper paste and stick on. Papier mâché is a slow process—do a few layers each day.

When the bowl is nearly thick enough, help your children to make the last few layers from strips of white butcher's paper.

When it is all dry, they can paint the inside and outside well with white acrylic paint. Kerenne says that large bright designs look great painted on the bowls and she gets the children to draw on their designs, first with a felt pen and then paint after. Maybe your children could colour-coordinate the bowl to your kitchen or family room décor for a cheap designer look!

RUBBER BAND BALL

A fun recycling activity that will also help develop your children's fine motor skills.

What You Need

- Rubber bands

What To Do

Every day we seem to get rubber bands around newspapers and mail, and they certainly can accumulate. Recycle them by making rubber band balls with your children. They will love a bouncing ball they made themselves.

Scrunch together a few rubber bands or even tie them up and begin stretching the others around this core as many times as necessary. Keep building it until it is the size you want. You can make lots together or your children and their friends might like to have a competition to see who can make the biggest—maybe an item for the *Guinness Book of Records*!

STAINED GLASS PICTURES

A way to use up old crayons to create beautiful, colourful pictures.

What You Need

- Old broken wax crayons • Cheese grater
- Grease proof paper • Iron

What To Do

Help your children grate old wax crayons into separate piles of colours.

They then make a design or picture on the waxed paper with the crayon gratings. Cover this with another piece of waxed paper and iron the two pieces together using a cool iron.

You can frame their creation or just Blu-Tack it on a window where the sun will shine through to give it a 'stained glass' window effect.

STAINED GLASS WINDOWS

Another 'stained glass' activity with cellophane scraps to help your children learn about colour mixing and making new colours.

What You Need

- Scraps of cellophane • Glue or sticky tape
- Scissors • Paper

What To Do

Your children may need help to fold a piece of paper three times. They then cut interesting shapes out of the sides of the paper. Open it up to see what they have made.

Now help your children glue or tape pieces of cellophane over the cut-out shapes for a very colourful effect. Hang these 'stained glass' pictures on their bedroom windows with the sun shining through. Perhaps you could visit a local church or cathedral, so they can see real stained glass windows.

STENCILS

Like most people, I buy a lot of the family's meat and chicken on styrofoam trays. Wash these up and save them because they make excellent stencils for the children to paint with.

What You Need

- Polystyrene trays • Pencils or pens • Paints
- Brushes • Scissors or a craft knife • Paper

What To Do

Have your children draw a simple design on the trays with a pencil or ball point pen. Use sharp-pointed scissors or a craft knife to cut out the design. Your children can then put the stencil over a piece of paper and paint inside the cut-out section. Carefully lift it off and admire their design.

Hint!

Make wrapping paper or cards with stencils. Perhaps heart shapes for Valentine's Day cards, bells, trees or holly leaves for Christmas wrapping paper or cards, or balloons for birthday wrapping paper. I'm sure your children will be able to think of lots more great ideas!

STREAMERS

6+

Children love making these colourful streamers for sports days, processions, or just to use as dancing props.

What You Need

- Pieces of dowel, rulers, chopsticks, or long unsharpened pencils
- Scissors • Strong glue • Crepe paper of all colours

What To Do

Help the children cut out long lengths of crepe paper. Choose a few strips of different colours and glue them from the end of a piece of dowel or ruler, pencil or chopstick.

Roll up the streamers tightly and then unwind. Show the children how to wave the streamers around to create colourful displays. They can hold a streamer in each hand and let the colours mix. Put on some dancing music out in the back yard and let the kids dance with their streamers.

Hint!

Streamers are great for school sports days, made in their school or house colours. Volunteer to go to your children's classroom the day before sports day, take all the makings and help the children make streamers in their own house colours. You'll be a very popular person.

TOOTHPICK MODELS

Children will spend hours modelling with toothpicks, matchsticks, playdough or plasticine. Bring out all these things on those wet, boring days and they will be happily occupied for ages (well, at least for long enough for you to read the paper and have a cup of coffee!).

What You Need

- Plasticine, clay or playdough • Toothpicks (for younger children you could substitute dead matcsticks or the brightly dyed matchsticks available at craft or junk stores)

What To Do

Show the children how to roll small balls of plasticine or playdough and then stick the toothpicks in them. Use the balls as the corner stones of the houses and other buildings they make. They can stick in lots of toothpicks to form the walls and then make doors, windows and roofs out of pieces of paper or cardboard.

Bring out some small props and they could make farms for their farm animals, houses for Lego or Duplo people or perhaps an airport or bridge for small planes and cars. They'll think of lots of creative ways to use the toothpicks once you get them started.

Don't forget to find the camera to take some photos of their wonderful creations before they fall to pieces. Who knows—you may have an architect in the family one day!

TWIG WEAVINGS

6+

Introduce your children to the concept of weaving with this fun activity.

What You Need

- Twigs 30–40 cm (12–16 in) long
- Pieces of wool, ribbon, strips of fabric etc.
- Sharp knife • Something to hang the weavings from

What To Do

Explain the concept of warps and weft to your children. Together, look at some loosely woven fabric such as hessian or linen so they understand.

Cut about 20 pieces of wool of equal length for the warp. Using the knife, cut notches in the sticks at equal distances so the wool doesn't slide. Tie the warp threads to the bottom and top sticks and, with another piece of wool, hang it to a door handle, a hook or a tree branch.

Anchor the bottom stick to a brick so it stays steady while your children are weaving. Your children then use the rest of the wool or other materials to make an interesting weaving. Later, they can cut the weaving off to use as a mat or hang it up in the frame.

BANKSIA MEN

*After the flowers have fallen from banksias, they leave behind woody cones.
Collect a few with the children to make some Banksia Men.*

What You Need

- Banksia cones • Gumnuts
- Small branches and pieces of wood
- PVA glue • Estapol

What To Do

Many of us were brought up on the fascinating adventures of Snugglepot and Cuddlepie and the big, bad Banksia Men of May Gibbs. Show your children how to make their own versions of Banksia Men.

Many coastal parts of Australia have wonderful areas of banksias. The group was named after Sir Joseph Banks, the botanist who sailed to Australia with Captain Cook in 1770 and was fascinated by our beautiful and unusual native plants.

Banksias grow spiky or fuzzy cone-like flowers which can be red, pink, orange or yellow in colour. After the flowers fall, gather some of the woody cones left to make the Banksia Men.

Glue on a few gumnuts for the eyes and mouths and the Banksia Men can be glued onto cut sections of wood or small branches. The children will be fascinated by the unique character of each man they make and they will have great fun naming them.

Don't forget to read May Gibb's stories together if the children aren't already familiar with them.

BATH FIZZ!

Help your children make some deliciously scented bath salts to use,
or give away as gifts. Add some excitement to bath time!

What You Need

- Bicarbonate of soda • A glass jar with a lid
- A measuring cup • Cornflour • Cream of tartar
- Essential oils such as lavender (available from health food stores)

What To Do

Measure three-quarters of a cup of bicarbonate of soda, two tablespoons of cornflour and half a cup of cream of tartar. Put them all into the jar and stir well, to mix and break up any lumps.

Add a few drops of essential oil or perfume and mix really well again.

When your children are in the bath, drop in spoonfuls of the bath salts. They are sure to love the fizzy sensation and the delicious smell!

BOX PUPPETS

Children love puppets. Help your children to make a marionette puppet that works really well, out of household junk.

What You Need

- A milk carton • Paper • String • Glue • Wooden sticks
- A pencil • Felt pens and other materials to decorate the puppet

What To Do

Help your children to make a hole in each side of the top part of the milk carton, for the puppet's arms. To make movable arms, wrap strips of paper tightly around a pencil and then glue the strips in place. Thread a long piece of string through the milk carton and then thread the paper cylinders onto the string to make arms on each side. Next, tie more strings onto the arms and attach them to the sticks that make the puppet work. You can make two legs in the same way.

The children will enjoy decorating the milk carton and finally attaching a string to the top of it to make the 'head' move. Tie the crossed sticks together and show them how to make the puppet move by moving the sticks.

Help them make a few marionette puppets and put on a puppet show together.

CITRUS PEEL JEWELLERY

7+

Your children can make some creative and individual jewellery from citrus fruit to give as gifts or for themselves. It's easy and fun!

What You Need

- Oranges, lemons, grapefruit, mandarins, limes
- String or thin leather thonging • Sharp knife
- Pencil or knitting needle

What To Do

Help your children cut interesting shapes from the citrus peel—they can eat the rest of the fruit or make some delicious juice afterwards.

Make holes in each piece of peel while it is still soft. Then leave it to dry. Flatten some pieces by leaving a weight on them while they are drying. Make cylindrical pieces by winding strips around the pencil or knitting needle.

When all the pieces are dry, your children can thread them onto string or the leather thonging. Make the designs different by alternating small beads (available from bead or craft shops).

DECORATIVE NATURAL NECKLACES

Older children will enjoy making these attractive necklaces using natural materials.

What You Need

• Wheat stalks • A mixture of seeds such as pumpkin, sunflower, bean, or melon • Fishing line or a strong button thread • Sharp needles • Spray-on or paint-on varnish

What To Do

First, the children cut up the wheat stalks into short lengths and begin threading. They can thread the seeds and stalks into attractively patterned necklaces.

When they have finished, show them how to coat their necklaces with spray-on or paint-on varnish.

FRAMED FLOWERS

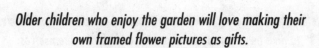

Older children who enjoy the garden will love making their own framed flower pictures as gifts.

What You Need

- Thick books • Flowers, leaves and grasses • Frames
- Good quality white or cream cardboard
- Latex adhesive or clear plastic adhesive spray

What To Do

Many flowers retain their colour and beauty when pressed, and make wonderful pictures. Cut the plant material the children wish to press on a dry day, so that it is not moist and dewy. Then place it inside a heavy book, between two pieces of blotting or kitchen paper. Position the book under a chair cushion or mattress, or under a pile of other heavy books. The length of time it takes plants to dry depends on the weather and the individual plant material, but check after two weeks.

Help the children position their dried flowers and other materials on the cardboard, which should be cut to size to fit the frame, with the border outlined with a light pencil. Smaller flowers or petals can be used to make decorative borders; rose leaves and ferns make very effective borders.

When the children are satisfied with their design, it is time to secure them in place with a little dab of the latex-based glue on the back of each flower or leaf or by spraying with the adhesive spray.

When the glue on the dried flowers is completely dry, place the pictures in the frames and secure. Choose simple and fairly light frames to ensure they don't detract from the delicate flower pictures. Many native plants dry very well and make interesting and effective pictures.

7+

GLITTER GIFT BOXES

Help your children to make some beautiful personalised gift boxes,
to give away on special occasions or keep for themselves.

What You Need

- Plain cardboard gift boxes (from craft store or
department store) • Newspapers • Acrylic paints
- Brushes • Pencils • PVA glue • Glitter

What To Do

Cover a table with newspapers (to protect it) and then let your children paint their gift boxes with the acrylic paint. Encourage them to draw interesting shapes such as stars and moons on the boxes. Once they have finished, leave the acrylic paint until it is quite dry.

Once the paint has dried, help your children to paint a thin layer of PVA glue over the areas on the boxes they want to cover with glitter. Then allow them to sprinkle glitter liberally over the PVA. Again, put leave the boxes to thoroughly dry—overnight is best.

When the boxes have dried, the children can blow of the excess glitter and their sparkling gift boxes are finished!

LET'S MODEL

*This modelling mixture is great for older children. They can use
it to make models that last forever.*

What You Need

- Plaster of Paris (available from hardware stores or craft suppliers)
- Plain flour • Water • Paint

What To Do

Your children can help you make up modelling mixture using one part plaster of Paris, three parts of flour and enough water to make a dough consistency.

This mixture will remain workable for about an hour. Your children will enjoy making models with the mixture. Dry the models in the sun until very firm and then the children can paint them.

Who knows, they may become sculptors one day!

MODELLING DOUGH

Here is another simple recipe for modelling dough.
It is perfect for making small jewellery and ornaments.

What You Need

• White bread • Glue • Lemon juice or eucalyptus oil

What To Do

Cut off the crusts from half a dozen slices of the bread and break into little pieces. Add two tablespoons of glue and the juice of half a lemon or a few drops of eucalyptus oil. Thoroughly mix the ingredients together, until the dough is ready for your children to use for modelling.

Your children will use their imaginations and make all kinds of little models with this dough, but beads are a favourite. If they are making beads, be sure any holes are made before the beads dry.

Once your children have finished making their creations, place the finished pieces on a tray covered with grease proof paper. The dough items will take at least two days to dry and should be turned frequently.

Later, your children will enjoy painting their creation with some acrylic or water paints.

ORANGE POMANDERS

Revive an old-fashioned craft by making fragrant pomander balls with your children.

What You Need

- Oranges with thin skins • Skewer or thin kebab stick
- Paper bag • Cloves • 1 tablespoon of cinnamon
- 1 tablespoon of orris powder (available from chemists)
- Tissue paper or kitchen paper • Ribbon

What To Do

Show the children how to make holes in the oranges with the skewers. Make holes all over and then insert a clove into each hole. Do this until the orange is totally covered with cloves.

Then, help the children combine the cinnamon and orris powder in a paper bag, and shake the oranges in the mixture until they are quite powdery. Wrap the oranges in the tissue paper, leave them in a warm place and in a month they will be ready.

Orange pomanders look great tied with Christmas ribbon. Grandmas and aunts will love one for a gift to hang in their cupboards!

PAPIER MÂCHÉ

A fun and creative long term project for older children that has lots of uses!

What You Need

- Non-toxic wallpaper paste
- Strips of newspaper about 4 cm (1 ½ in) wide • Balloon

What To Do

Blow up the balloon and simply dip strips of newspaper into the wallpaper paste and place on the balloon.

Papier mâché must be done slowly and allowed to dry well between each application so it won't mildew. Don't apply more than three or four layers at a time. Peg the balloon on the clothesline so it dries quickly. When the papier mâché is strong enough, burst the balloon inside with a pin and it can be cut and used for something special.

Your children can make some masks out of their papier mâché, or a collection of funny animals.

POTPOURRI

*Help your children store the flower scents of spring and summer blossoms
by turning them into beautiful, fragrant potpourri.*

What You Need

- Lots of scented flowers—roses, carnations, annuals, freesias, lavender etc.
- Orris powder (available from chemists) • Mixed spice or allspice
- Brown sugar • Salt • Large storage bottle with a lid

What To Do

Early one warm morning, gather all the flowers you will need for this project (at least enough for about three cupfuls of petals). Stand the flowers in a bucket of water for a day. Then strip off all the petals and put them in a shady place on newspaper for a few days. Turn them at least once a day. When the petals are dry and stiff, you can make the potpourri.

Mix together:

1 tablespoon orris powder
5 tablespoons spices
1 tablespoon sugar

Put a layer of petals in a large jar and sprinkle on lots of salt. Then sprinkle over a small handful of spices. Do this in layers until the petals are all used up.

Stir every couple of days for about three weeks. By then the oils and scents will have mingled. Potpourri is great in bowls in the house as room freshener, or your children might like to give it away for gifts. When it begins to lose its fragrance, add a few drops of an essential oil like boronia or lavender to refresh it.

7+

POTPOURRI POUCHES

*Your children can use the potpourri they made in the last activity to make these pouches.
They make excellent gifts, or they can use them themselves.*

What You Need

- Fine squares of fabric such as lawn or muslin
- Alternatively, use ladies' or children's hankies
- Pinking shears • Rubber bands
- Fine satin ribbon • Potpourri

What To Do

Potpourri pouches are best made out of doors so any spilt potpourri can simply be swept or hosed into the garden.

If you are using fabric rather than hankies, show the children how to cut the fabric into squares using the pinking shears. The serrated edges look most attractive.

Then the children simply spread out a hanky or fabric square, measure out three tablespoons or so of potpourri onto the hanky and twist the bottom of the hanky to form a little sack.

Help them wind a rubber band around the twist in the hanky until it is tight and then tie some ribbon over the rubber band to hide it.

Potpourri pouches are perfect to put in drawers to give your clothes a lovely scent, or tie them to coat hangers to add perfume to your wardrobe.

PRESSED FLOWER CARDS

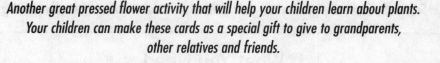

7+

Another great pressed flower activity that will help your children learn about plants. Your children can make these cards as a special gift to give to grandparents, other relatives and friends.

What You Need

- Flowers • Telephone books
- Absorbent paper—kitchen paper or blotting paper
- Cardboard • Pencils

What To Do

Gather small flowers from the garden—preferably using ones the size of a five cent or ten cent piece. Some flowers press better than others, so you will have to experiment.

There are many flower presses on the market and if your children really become interested in this hobby, one of them would make a lovely gift. However, old telephone books work just as well. Press the flowers between the kitchen paper and help the children place them between the pages. Leave at least 20 pages between each set of flowers. Stack some heavy books or even bricks on top of the telephone books and leave for a couple of weeks.

Help your children cut out the card, draw oval or round shapes on the front and creatively arrange the pressed flowers. Glue the flowers in place with dots of craft glue. Leaves, a little lace and ribbon, and some grasses can all be glued with the flowers for a pretty effect.

7+

ROLLER PRINTING

Search the house and garden with your children to find lots of items for roller printing.

What You Need

- An assortment of items to roll
- Acrylic or poster paint • Paper

What To Do

Have a look around with the children and see what you can all find for roller printing. You may like to use:

Hair rollers

Cotton spools

A cob of corn

String glued onto a can with PVA glue

Kitchen utensils such as scone cutters

Ribbon or string wrapped and glued around a bottle

Shapes cut out of cardboard toilet or lunch wrap rolls

Cardboard shapes glued onto a rolling pin

Round toys

Tennis or golf balls

Set the children up outside with painting smocks or old shirts over their clothes. They will have lots of fun making different patterns with all the rolling implements you have found.

SCREEN PAINTING

Another fun, but messy, screen painting activity that is best done outdoors.

What You Need

- A piece of fine plastic gutter guard or other fine screen
- A shirt box or baking tray of similar size • Paper
- Old toothbrush • Cardboard • Pencils
- Scissors • Acrylic or poster paints

What To Do

Help your children to make some interesting stencil shapes. Draw stars, moons, animals etc. onto the cardboard and then cut them out.

Now cut the gutter guard or screen so it is big enough to fit over the box or baking tray. Place a piece of paper in the box and lay some of the cut-out shapes on top of it. Show the children how to dip the toothbrush in paint and then brush it across the screen so that the paint splatters onto the paper. If you are only using one toothbrush, have a container of clean water to wash it between colours. If you have a few old toothbrushes put one in each pot of colour.

The children will love making these screen paintings and observing how the part covered by the shapes they cut out stays free of paint.

7+

SHOE BOX DIORAMA

A special way to display small objects or make a favourite story come to life.

What You Need

• A shoe box • Playdough, plasticine or Blu-tac • Ice block sticks

What To Do

Help your children cut out the side of the shoe box. Decide what scene you are going to make and think of what you can use. They could paint the sides and back of the shoe box first, with colours suitable for the scene they are going to make.

Small mirrors or cellophane make excellent ponds and crepe paper can be used for trees and grass. Ice block sticks can be decorated for people and the playdough, plasticine or Blu-Tack can hold objects in place.

Your children may like to make a farm, a dinosaur world or perhaps their favourite fairy tale or nursery rhyme!

STABILES

Your children will have lots of fun being creative and arranging different objects, when making stabiles.

What You Need

- Clay, plasticine or polystyrene for the base
- Toothpicks, ice block sticks, pipe cleaners, pasta, polystyrene pieces, leaves, flowers
- Coloured paper or cardboard
- Sticky tape or Blu-Tack

What To Do

Using the clay, plasticine or a piece of polystyrene as a base, your children poke the sticks, pipe cleaners or toothpicks into it.

They then decorate them with leaves, flowers or shapes. If they need to secure them, use small blobs of Blu-Tack or sticky tape.

Stabiles are also fun to make at Christmas time, using pictures cut from old cards, bits of tinsel and small decorations. Make one with your children for a centrepiece for the Christmas dinner table.

7+

TENNIS BALL PAINTING

Children love watching the patterns and new colours form as the balls roll around.

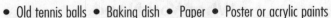

What You Need

- Old tennis balls • Baking dish • Paper • Poster or acrylic paints
- Plastic yoghurt, margarine, or take-away containers • Dessert spoons

What To Do

Lay a sheet of paper inside the baking dish and spoon a little paint of each colour into the plastic containers. Then put a tennis ball into each container and the children can use the spoon to cover it with paint.

Then they lift a couple of the balls into the baking dish and tilt it from side to side so that the balls roll around, mixing the paints, making new colours and spreading them into interesting shapes and patterns.

If you only use primary colours this will help teach younger children about how new colours are made. Yellow and red makes orange. Yellow and blue makes green. And red and blue makes purple.

Keep the paper so that the children can use it for very individual gift wrap.

WIRE SCULPTURES

*Your children will enjoy creating with a different medium
to form unusual but very effective sculptures.*

What You Need

- Wire—buy wire that is not too thick, so your children can still bend
and shape it easily—florists have a variety of wire for floral art
- Wire cutters • Strips of white fabric • PVA glue • Acrylic paints • Blu-Tack

What To Do

This activity is best done on an outside table covered with a plastic or vinyl cloth, as it is fairly messy.

Help your children shape their wire into interesting shapes—perhaps human figures, animals, or any shape they fancy. Use a blob of Blu-Tack to stand or sit the figure or figures upright.

Use the wire cutters to cut the wire into different lengths and to trim neatly. The next step is to dilute the PVA glue half and half with water in a large, shallow bowl. Cut the fabric into 2 cm ($^4/_5$ in) wide strips, dip it into the glue mixture and then wrap it around the wire. The children continue doing this until the wrapping is as thick as they want it to be.

Leave the figures until they are completely dry and then the children will enjoy painting them. Use the Blu-Tack to stand the figures somewhere for display. Everyone will be impressed by the children's creativity.

CHICKEN WIRE SCULPTURES

*If your children have enjoyed making sculptures from wire,
they will enjoy the challenge of an even bigger project!*

What You Need

- Chicken wire (available from hardware stores, fencing contractors)
- Wire cutters • PVA glue • Lots of newspaper • Acrylic or house paint
- Brushes • Scissors • Masking tape

What To Do

Decide together what the project will be; perhaps a figure or an animal, a dinosaur or a space alien. The children will have no trouble thinking of something creative and unusual.

Wearing gardening gloves, bend the chicken wire into the shape they want. Cover any pieces that may stick out with some masking tape, as the wire can be very sharp.

The next step involves pasting papier mâché all over the wire. This is done by diluting the PVA glue half and half with water. Then dip large pieces of newspaper into the glue mixture and paste them over the wire until it is completely covered. This stage may take a few days as the paper needs to dry well between coats.

The children will love painting and decorating their wonderful creation when it is completely dry.

COLOURFUL BOTTLES

8+

You can help your children to make these colourful bottles. They make useful and decorative storage, or the children can give them away for gifts.

What You Need

- Bottles of different shapes and sizes • Masking tape
- Metallic spray paints (available from hardware and craft stores)
- Scissors • Newspaper

What To Do

Help your children cut out shapes from the masking tape and use them to decorate the bottles. Stars, moons, hearts, fish, shells, flowers and geometric shapes all look great.

Next, cover an area well with newspaper and help them to carefully spray the bottles. When the paint is dry, peel off the masking tape to reveal the interesting patterns they have made.

Your children can name their work (like all artists) by writing their name on the bottom of their bottle art!

DOT PAINTINGS

What You Need

- Drawing paper (computer paper, etc.)
- Paints and a fine brush (only primary colours)
- Coloured pencils (red, blue, yellow)
- Fine pointed felt pens

What To Do

Encourage your children to draw or paint using only a technique of tiny dots of primary colours. Your children may prefer to lightly pencil in the drawing and then colour it with the dots.

Show your children some Impressionist paintings that use this technique, such as ones by Van Gogh, Seurat, Monet and others. Your local library will have lots of art books you can borrow to look at with your children, or perhaps you are lucky enough to live near an art gallery that you can visit together.

As your children can only use dots of primary colours, they will have to think carefully about what dots to mix together to produce other colours, perhaps yellow and red to produce orange.

DRY FOOD JEWELLERY

8+

Older children will enjoy making unusual jewellery from dried foods.

What You Need

- Dried fruit, such as dried apple rings
- Macaroni • Needle and thread
- Paper clips • Clear varnish and a brush

What To Do

Help your children work out a pattern with the dried fruit, beans and macaroni. Then they can carefully sew through the dried fruit, the macaroni.

When the necklace is finished, help them attach a paper clip to each end so they can link together to fasten the necklace. They can even make matching earrings and a bracelet.

Finally, varnish the jewellery. Varnish adds to the appearance, as well as making the jewellery last longer too.

DYEING

*Show your children how lovely dyes can be made with
plants from your own pantry or garden.*

What You Need

- A large saucepan • T-shirt or fabric • Pair of pantyhose
- Natural substances to dye with • Water
- A wooden spoon • Sewing cotton or a thin string

What To Do

Children are always amazed at the dyes that can be made from plants in our own gardens. Most plants have dye colour; roots, flowers, bark, leaves and berries will all yield colour. Other natural substances that make very successful dyes are brown onion skins, coffee, tea, curry powder and red cabbage. Gum leaves will give a wonderful range of colours depending on the mordant (the chemical you use for fixing the colour in the fabric). Some common mordants include alum, iron, chrome, copper, tin, oxalic acid and tannic acid.

To dye a T-shirt, first wash and rinse it very well if it is brand new to remove any starch or finish that is in the garment. Put the leaves, flowers, etc. that you are using to dye in the pantyhose and tie them up well with the string or cotton, so none escape. Fill the saucepan with water and add the pantyhose. Then add the T-shirt or fabric and bring to the boil, stirring all the time. Turn the heat down and simmer, stirring occasionally. Lift out the garment from time to time so you can see if the colour is deep enough.

When the T-shirt is coloured sufficiently, rinse well in cold water and leave to dry. Cotton garments dye very successfully. Experiment first with white cotton to see the colours you will obtain.

ETCHINGS

Older children will love this new way to make colourful drawings.

What You Need

• Paper • Crayons • Matchsticks, spoons, paint brushes

What To Do

Show your children how to fill a whole piece of paper with every colour crayon except black. It is important that this first layer of colour is quite thick, so make sure your children press down heavily and apply the colour all over. Next, take a black crayon and, using it on its side, cover all the colours with black.

Then show the children how to use a pointed implement such as a spoon handle, paint brush end or match stick, to scratch a picture on the paper. The black is scratched away, revealing the bright colours beneath it!

GOD'S EYES

Show your children how to make this simple form of folk art.
God's Eyes originated in South America and were religious symbols.

What You Need

- Brightly coloured wool
- Two sticks about 15–20 cm (6–8 in) long

What To Do

Hold the sticks while your children tie them together to form a cross. Then show them how to hold the two sticks together where they join and loop the wool around the first stick close to the knot. Wrap the wool first around one stick, then the next, to keep forming X's. Remind them to keep turning the God's Eye as they work.

Change wool often, tying one colour to the next to make it as bright as possible. Finish the God's Eye off by tying the wool to the stick. Bells and tassels are often added to make them even more colourful and decorative.

Your children might like to make a few God's Eyes to decorate a wall in their bedroom.

HERB POSIES

Children love smelling different types of herbs.
Show them how to make a herb posy.

What You Need

• Herbs and lavender flowers • Rubber bands • Pretty ribbons

What To Do

Take the children outside and gather some sprigs of different herbs from your herb garden. Posies are traditionally round in shape and the children will have to cut the stems so they have a mixture of lengths. Lavender smells wonderful and the flowers add colour to the posy, but other herb flowers such as the bright red-pink of pineapple sage and dainty thyme flowers also look great. Use a variety of herbs with different leaf shapes for the posy, such as the spiky leaves of rosemary contrasted with the soft round leaves of basil. Parsley looks pretty and soft around the edges. The children will enjoy selecting a variety of leaf shapes.

Wrap a rubber band firmly around the posy and then tie a pretty ribbon over the rubber band. Try a herb posy as a gift or keep one or two around the home and enjoy the wonderful natural scent of herbs.

8+

INSECT BROOCHES

Older children with some basic sewing skills will enjoy making insect brooches to decorate a plain sweatshirt or T-shirt, or to give to special friends as a gift.

What You Need

- Oddments of felt and lace • Chalk • Safety pins
- Mug • Old pantyhose • Craft glue • Sequins
- Scissors • Felt pen • Needle and thread

What To Do

Begin by making a ladybird. Draw a small circle on some red or orange felt and help your children cut it out. Show them how to sew large running stitches as close to the edge of the fabric as possible. Next, help them gather up the running stitches and put some pieces of cut-up pantyhose in the centre. Pull the stitches up really tight and tie off the ends. Mould the fabric into a long oval shape and sew carefully over the gap to close it. Your children will enjoy marking on the ladybird's spots with a black felt pen. Add a safety pin to attach it.

To make a bee, follow the same steps using black felt or black fabric. Then glue on with the craft glue some strips of yellow felt to make the bee's stripes. Scraps of lace make great wings and attach a safety pin at the back.

To make a butterfly brooch, use purple or pink felt or fabric and add some beautiful lacy wings and glue on some bright sequins. Again, add a safety pin at the back.

KNOCK-KNOCK CARDS

Help your children make their own joke cards to give to their friends.
Lots of creative fun and saves money too!

What You Need

• Paper • Scissors • Craft knife • Glue • Felt pens

What To Do

Measure two blank pieces of paper about 20 cm by 15 cm (8 in by 6 in). Your children should then carefully cut them out and then fold them in half.

Draw a square about 5 cm by 5 cm (2 in by 2 in) on the front of one of the cards and then cut it out on three sides so it opens like a door. It is easier to cut this with a craft knife, but if your children want to do it themselves, start the cut with the knife and let them do the rest with scissors.

Next, glue the uncut card to the inside of this card, except where the door is. When it is dry your children can decorate the card with a knock-knock joke and put the answer inside the card.

LAVENDER POTPOURRI

Here is another recipe for potpourri, for older children to try. If they have made the lavender sachets in this book, or the earlier recipe for potpourri, they will enjoy the challenge of making this one.

What You Need

- 3 cups of lavender flowers • 2 cups of rose petals • Grated peel of 2 lemons • 1 cup of lemon balm leaves or other 'lemony' leaves such as lemon-scented gum or leptospermum leaves • 1/4 cup of orris powder (available from chemists or health food stores) • 4 drops of essential lavender oil • Sealed container

What To Do

Help your children to strip the flowers and leaves for the potpourri. Then mix them with the lemon peel, or lemon-scented leaves. Finally sprinkle on the orris powder and the lavender oil and leave in the sealed container for six weeks.

Put the potpourri into pretty open bowls in different rooms of the house and enjoy the wonderful perfume. Containers of potpourri make great gifts; the children will enjoy making some for their teachers at Christmas time or for Teacher's Day.

MOSAIC TABLES

Older children will enjoy a more complicated project like this one,
with a little help from Mum or Dad.

What You Need

• A piece of marine ply which is the desired size and shape for the
top of the table • Screw in legs • A selection of ceramic tiles • Tile adhesive
• Grout (all the products listed here are available from hardware stores and tile shops)

What To Do

Borrow some books about ancient Greek and Roman mosaics to teach your children a little of the history of this wonderful art form. They may even like to copy some of the simpler ancient designs!

Paint around the edge of the piece of wood before you start. Use a colour that will tone with the tiles your children have chosen.

Put the tiles into a couple of strong plastic bags and help your children hit them firmly with a hammer to break them into small pieces. Now they will have the challenge of making patterns for the table top with the small pieces of tiles. When they have the tiles in place help them glue them, moving only a few at a time.

Leave to dry completely and then help your children to grout the tiles to fill in the gaps. Finally, screw in the legs of the table and the mosaic table is finished.

8+

NOODLE NAMES

Children love eating pasta—and they also love creating art works with it!
However, like many messy art activities, this one is best done outdoors.

What You Need

• Pasta of various shapes • Strong glue such as PVA • Cardboard

What To Do

Children love names on their bedroom doors and messages too. Decide on the message your children want to create. Then cut some cardboard into the shape they want. They can paint on the letters carefully with the glue.

Next, they position the pasta onto the glue before it dries. Let the pasta dry for a day or so. Then punch holes in the corner of each sign and thread with string or ribbon to hang on the children's bedroom door knobs.

Hint!

Pasta can even be coloured with paint and left to dry if you want to use coloured pasta for this activity. Or you can buy different coloured pasta.

PAPER JEWELLERY

8+

Older children will enjoy creating their own jewellery from colourful paper to match an outfit for a special event.

What You Need

- Colourful paper—can be bought from the newsagents, but old wrapping paper, advertising brochures, envelopes and brown paper work well too.
- Glue • Scissors • Pencil or knitting needles

What To Do

To make a colourful bracelet, take two long strips of contrasting paper. Glue the ends together at right angles and fold one piece over the other, then over the other and so on (your children will probably have made Christmas streamers using this method). Glue the ends together when the bracelet is finished. This bracelet expands like a concertina so the children will be able to slip it over an arm easily.

Make a matching necklace by cutting long, thin paper triangles. Begin with the wide end and roll the triangle as tightly as possible around a pencil or knitting needles. Put a spot of glue at the end to hold it in place. Thread the colourful beads onto some wool or cord.

Instant chic!

PASTA PHOTO FRAMES

Here is another fun activity with pasta for older children. Help them make some interesting photo frames for their room, or to give as gifts.

What You Need

- Strong cardboard
- Strong glue such as craft glue or PVA
- Variety of pasta shapes (bows, twirls, etc.)
- Gold or silver metallic spray paint

What To Do

Select the photos first for size, then cut a piece of strong card to double the size you need. Be sure to leave room for a border. Score with a knife and ruler, and then fold in half carefully. Cut out the section for the photo, leaving a border of at least 5 cm (2 in).

Help your children decorate the frame with the pasta shapes and strong glue. Leave it to dry for several hours, or overnight. If you wish, spray with the gold or silver paint, but make sure you do this outside on a still day.

Glue the photo in the frame and then glue the cardboard together. Attach a small piece of strong card at the back so your frame can stand up.

POMPOMS

Older children will be able to make lots of fun animals once they have mastered the knack of making woollen pompoms.

What You Need

- Scissors • Cardboard • Needle and cotton
- Wool • Strong glue such as PVA

What To Do

Help your children cut two round circles from cardboard—whatever size they want the finished pompoms to be. Next, cut a small hole in the centre of each cardboard circle. Your children then wrap wool around and around the circles until the centre hole is completely full.

With the point of the scissors, cut the wool between the two circles. Take a length of wool and help your children tie it between the circles and knot firmly to hold the pompom together. Finally, cut away the cardboard, trim the tie and the pompom is finished!

Your children could join lots of pompoms together to make a caterpillar, make a pompom teddy or mouse, or attach one to hat elastic and a paper cup and use it for a catch game. Pompoms also make great decorations on hats and clothes.

TIE-DYED T-SHIRTS

Help your older children dye their own very fashionable tie-dyed T-shirts.

What You Need

- White cotton T-shirts • A large non-aluminium pot for dyeing
- Commercial fabric dyes • String • Large wooden spoon
- Water • Towels

What To Do

Spread newspapers all over an outdoor table and cover the children and yourself with painting smocks or large old shirts.

Help them tie the T-shirt in tight knots or tie pieces of the string around parts. Make up the dye according to the directions on the packet. Use the wooden spoon to stir the T-shirts around so they are well covered.

After dyeing, help your children rinse the T-shirts very thoroughly in cold water. Then untie the knots or string and rinse again very well. Squeeze out any excess water and spread the shirts on a thick towel to dry.

If the children wish, they can re-tie or use more string to re-knot the T-shirts and dye them with another colour. When they have finished dyeing, help them rinse again well and dry the T-shirts. Cover with a clean cloth and iron to help set the dye.

Your children will love wearing their trendy tie-dyed T-shirts. Why don't you get them to dye one for you?

T-SHIRT ART

Here is another creative T-shirt activity for your children to try.
They will proudly wear a T-shirt that they have decorated themselves.

What You Need

- Plain T-shirt • Fabric crayons (available at fabric and craft shops)
- White paper • Iron and ironing board • Tea towel

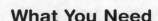

What To Do

Suggest to your children that they work out their design before drawing it with the fabric crayons. They then draw the design on the white paper, colouring as heavily as they can.

Put a tea towel on the ironing board and pull the front of the T-shirt through the board (this will stop the design going through to the other side of the T-shirt).

Place the drawing face-down on the fabric and do the ironing yourself. Press down with a warm iron all over the design (don't move the iron back and forward or the design will blur). The crayon picture will transfer to the T-shirt.

Remove the piece of paper and see how the wax has melted the design onto the T-shirt. Your children may also like to decorate the back of their T-shirt!

TWIG FRAMES

*The country look is still very popular and twig frames are very easy,
as well as cheap and fun, for the children to make.*

What You Need

- Twigs of different size, colour and texture • A cardboard box
- Strong scissors • PVA glue • Ruler and pencil

What To Do

Cut out the bottom of the cardboard box with the children and, when they decide what size they would like their frames to be, measure out a rectangle or square shape for the back. Cut two the same size. Then cut out the middle of one and glue it on the top of the other, leaving the top unglued. This space at the top is where you slide your photo or picture into the frame when it is finished.

Now the children will enjoy cutting their twigs to size and gluing them onto the frame. It looks more interesting if they cut the twigs into different lengths. Encourage the children to choose a variety of textures and colours in the twigs, for interest.

When the twigs are dry, help them cut out a large triangle from the strong cardboard. Make a fold in the long side of the triangle and then glue it onto the back of the twig frame so it can stand. If they want to hang it, screw in a couple of tiny cup hooks and tie some fine string or fishing line between them to hang the frame.

Your children's twig frames will be much admired by everyone.

WOOL BALLOONS

8+

Help your children make some wool or string balloons to hang from the ceilings in your house, or at school.

What You Need

- Balloons • Plaster of Paris
- Old container or bucket
- Lengths of colourful wool or string

What To Do

Cover a table outside with some newspaper or a plastic or vinyl cloth. The children can each blow up a balloon.

Mix up some of the plaster with water in an old container.

The children soak the wool in the plaster and wrap it around the balloon. Use lots and lots of lengths of wool. When they have done enough, leave the balloon until the string hardens. Then burst the balloon and pull it through a hole.

Wool balloons are great for parties and special occasions.

FOOD FUN

BARBECUED FRUIT KEBABS

Kids who love food on skewers will really enjoy these yummy fruit kebabs—and they will be eager to help prepare them!

What You Need

- A variety of fresh fruit—bananas, strawberries, pineapple, mangoes, stone fruit—or tinned fruit if unavailable
- Wooden satay sticks soaked in water for an hour
- 2 tablespoons melted butter • 2 tablespoons orange juice
- 2 tablespoons brown sugar • Basting brush

What To Do

The children will enjoy threading equal sized pieces of fresh or tinned fruit onto the satay sticks.

Combine the butter, sugar, and orange juice to form a basting sauce.

Cook the fruit kebabs on a barbecue plate (low heat) for 5–10 minutes, brushing frequently with the basting sauce.

These fruit kebabs are delicious served with ice-cream, cream or yoghurt.

CHEESY BALLS

A delicious, easy, savoury treat you can make with the children.

What You Need

- 1 tablespoon butter • $1\frac{1}{2}$ cups self raising flour
- 1 cup instant oats • 1 cup milk • 1 cup grated Cheddar cheese

What To Do

Show the children how to rub the butter into the flour until it resembles crumbs. Next they can grate the cheese and add it to the flour and butter mixture. Then add the oats and milk, and mix well. Children will enjoy rolling the mixture into small balls.

Place the cheesy balls on a well greased scone tray and bake at 200 degrees C (400 F) for 10–15 minutes until golden brown. Delicious warm but also great cold. Makes about 15.

COCONUT MACAROONS

Children will love making these yummy bikkies and the whole family will love eating them.

What You Need

- 2 cups desiccated coconut • 1 cup castor sugar
- 2 tablespoons cornflour • Pinch salt • 2 eggs

What To Do

First, help your children to measure all the dry ingredients into a mixing bowl. Next beat the eggs well and add to the dry ingredients. Mix them together well. Grease your biscuit trays and cover with baking paper, as macaroons tend to stick to the tray.

Place teaspoonfuls of the mixture onto the trays, leaving room for the macaroons to spread.

Bake 150 degrees C (300 F) for 15–20 minutes.

Makes about 24.

COCONUT RUM BALLS

Make some Rum Balls with your children for the family or to give as gifts on special occasions, like Christmas time. Great for your children's teachers, the neighbours—our milkman even got some last year!

What You Need

- 9 wheat cereal biscuits • 1 can condensed milk • 2 dessertspoons cocoa
- $^1/_2$ cup minced or finely chopped sultanas • 2 tablespoons rum
- Extra coconut for rolling

What To Do

First, your children crush the cereal biscuits with their hands or a rolling pin, in a large bowl. Then add all the other ingredients. The sultanas are best minced in a mincer (about the only time I use mine) or they can be finely chopped—you will have to help with this step.

Mix very well. Your children then roll teaspoonfuls in their clean hands (make hand-washing a prerequisite for cooking). Then they roll the ball in the extra coconut.

The Rum Balls make a decorative gift wrapped in cellophane and tied with ribbon.

JELLY FRUIT FLUMMERY

5+

I don't know where the word 'flummery' comes from but children love these delicious fluffy desserts, especially if they have helped make them.

What You Need

- 1 packet jelly crystals in your children's favourite flavour • ¹/₂ cup castor sugar
- Fruit—chopped bananas, pineapple or kiwi fruit pieces or passionfruit pulp
- 1 egg • 1 cup milk

What To Do

Your children can help stir the jelly crystals in one cup of hot water to dissolve them thoroughly. Stand the jelly until it's cool but not set. Add one cup of cold water from the fridge.

Let your children beat the egg with the sugar until nice and frothy and add the milk. Help them cut up the fruit and add to the jelly mixture. Then add the beaten mixture, stirring thoroughly together.

Put the jelly fruit flummery into a pretty bowl and put into the fridge to set.

A favourite dessert for young and old. Makes enough for six.

FRIED RICE

A healthy meal to cook with your children that all the family will enjoy.

What You Need

- 1¹/₂ cups rice • Water • 1 onion • 2 eggs
- 4 bacon rashers or slices of ham
- Frozen peas • Other vegetables the family likes
e.g. corn, capsicum, etc. • Soy sauce • Oil for cooking

What To Do

Bring about six cups of water to the boil and add the rice. When it is cooked, pour into a colander, let it drain and cool. Your children will be interested in the difference between a cooked and uncooked grain of rice.

Your children can help you chop up the onion, bacon and any other vegies you want to add. Add some oil to a pan and cook the onion and bacon, then remove.

Let your children break the eggs carefully into a bowl and mix together with a fork. Pour into the fry pan and let it cook like an omelette. Cut into pieces and add the cooked rice, bacon, onion and the rest of the ingredients. Mix together and all enjoy.

I find my child (who is a fairly picky eater, like many six-year-olds) really enjoys eating the meals he has helped to prepare.

MALTY BALLS

A delicious and healthy snack that you and your children can make together.

What You Need

- 1 cup skim milk powder • $\frac{1}{2}$ cup powdered milk • 2 cups corn flakes
- $\frac{1}{2}$ cup sultanas • $\frac{1}{4}$ cup coconut • 1 teaspoon carob or cocoa
- $\frac{1}{2}$ teaspoon vanilla • Water or fruit juice to bind

What To Do

Combine all the dry ingredients in a large bowl. Gradually add enough water or juice to combine.

Your children will enjoy rolling teaspoonfuls of the mixture in extra coconut. Keep the malty balls chilled.

Great for a picnic or a health snack at home!

MARINATED CHICKEN WINGS

These chicken wings are absolutely delicious, easy enough for the children to prepare with minimal adult supervision, and great for family picnics.

What You Need

- 2 kg (4lb) chicken wings (or substitute drumsticks if preferred)
- 2 cloves crushed garlic • 2 teaspoons grated ginger
- $\frac{1}{2}$ cup soy sauce • 2 teaspoons sugar
- 2 tablespoons sherry • 2 tablespoons oil
- 2 tablespoons honey

What To Do

The children can combine all the ingredients and mix by shaking well in a well sealed container.

Spread the chicken wings out in a large baking dish and pour the marinade over them. Refrigerate overnight or for a few hours.

Bake in a moderate oven, turning frequently for about an hour or until the wings are well cooked.

These chicken wings can also be cooked with great success on a barbecue plate at a fairly low temperature so they don't burn.

POTATO FRITTERS

A favourite recipe from my childhood that your children will enjoy helping to make and eat!

What You Need

- 3 medium sized potatoes • 2 beaten eggs
- $\frac{1}{2}$ cup plain flour • $\frac{1}{2}$ teaspoonful salt

What To Do

Peel the potatoes and then help your children to grate them into a colander. Rinse and squeeze out the excess liquid. Next, break the eggs into a mixing bowl and let your children beat them with a fork or whisk.

Add the potatoes to the eggs and then the flour and salt. Let the children mix them well. Shape into fritters. Add a small amount of cooking oil to a hot frypan and cook until golden brown. Makes 10–15.

SESAME SNAPS

A healthy, chewy snack that children adore.

What You Need

- $^3/_4$ cup honey • $^1/_2$ cup sunflower seeds
- $^1/_2$ cup skim milk powder • 1 cup sesame seeds
- $^1/_2$ cup shredded coconut

What To Do

Your children can help collect and measure out the ingredients needed for this recipe.

Bring the honey to the boil and then add all the other ingredients. You will have to do the pouring and mixing because the mixture is so hot.

Pour the mixture into a flat dish and pop it into the fridge to set. When it's cold, slice it into rectangles. Store in an airtight container in the fridge.

BAKED APPLES

A yummy dessert your children will enjoy making
(with a little adult help) for the whole family.

What You Need

These quantities are for one apple—it's a good maths lesson for your children to work out how much is needed for an apple per family member.

- 1 Granny Smith cooking apple • 1 teaspoon crushed nuts
- $\frac{1}{2}$ teaspoon sultanas • $\frac{1}{2}$ teaspoon coconut • 1 tablespoon honey

What To Do

Wash the apple and carefully core it with an apple corer, making sure you don't make the hole go through to the other side or all the delicious filling will dribble out. Fill the centre with the crushed nuts, sultanas and coconut. If any of your children are under 5 years old it's best to leave out the crushed nuts, in case they choke.

Next, let your children dribble the honey over the sides and into the centre of the apple. Bake the apples on a tray or in an oven-proof dish at 200 degrees C (400 F) for 45 minutes.

Delicious served with ice-cream.

7+

BARBECUED CORN ON THE COB

Corn on the cob is always delicious, but it's even yummier cooked outside on the barbecue. It's one vegetable the children will always eat.

What You Need

- Unpeeled corn cobs • Water • Butter
- Seasoning as desired • Aluminium foil

What To Do

Select tender, juicy cobs of corn at the greengrocer's shop or supermarket by pulling back the husks and making sure the kernels are young and fresh.

Help the children peel back the husks from the corn a little and remove the top silk. They then have to pull the husks back over the corn and soak in water for about an hour.

Wrap the corn, still in the husks, in foil and place on the coils or on the grill of the barbecue.

Turn regularly and cook for about 5 minutes each side. As the corn will be very hot, unwrap and de-husk using oven mitts. Season with salt, pepper and butter as desired. Yum!

FAMILY BOILED FRUIT CAKE

I think this recipe originally came from the Nursing Mother's Organisation, a wonderful group to which I belonged when my son was smaller.

What You Need

- 375 g (12 oz) mixed fruit
- 425 g (13.5 oz) tin crushed pineapple drained—reserve liquid
- 1 cup pineapple liquid with water added to make up quantity
- 125 g (4 oz) butter • 125 g (4 oz) sugar • 1 teaspoon mixed spice
- 1 teaspoon bicarb soda • 2 well-beaten eggs
- 125 g (4 oz) plain flour (wholemeal can be used, if desired)
- 125 g (4 oz) self raising flour

What To Do

Grease and line a 20 cm (8 in) square tin. Help your children place the fruit, water, butter, sugar and spice in a large saucepan. Now you can bring it to the boil, then simmer gently for a few minutes. Allow to cool.

Stir in the remaining ingredients, including crushed pineapple, and mix well.

Pour the mixture into the tin and bake in a preheated oven at 180 degrees C (350 F) for 1¹/₂ hours, reducing the heat to 160 degrees C (325 F) after 15 minutes.

The children will enjoy helping make this cake as there are lots of opportunities for measuring, mixing, pouring and even cutting the lining paper. Most of all they will love eating it, especially at a family picnic.

7+

HERBED VINEGARS

*Help the children make some delicious herbed vinegars
to use at home or to give away as special gifts.*

What You Need

- Herbs from the garden • Glass bottles with lids
(suitable bottles can be bought cheaply from discount stores)
- Good quality white wine vinegar • Labels • Coloured felt pens

What To Do

Go for a walk in the garden with your children and pick a selection of herbs to use. Good herbs for vinegars are rosemary, sage, thyme and marjoram.

Clean the bottles very well. Then the children can trim some herbs and add the sprigs to the bottles. Help them fill the bottles with vinegar and put the lids on tightly.

Next, the children can decorate some labels with pretty designs and write the names of the herbs in the vinegar on the labels.

Give the herbed vinegars away or use them up quickly for cooking. They are also excellent in delicious salad dressings.

WORLD'S GREATEST MEATBALLS

Meatballs are always popular for barbecues and this recipe is so easy that the children will be able to prepare them with just a little help from you.

What You Need

- 500 g (1 lb) mince • 1 onion finely diced • 1 clove garlic
- $^1/_2$ cup grated carrot • $^1/_2$ cup rolled oats • 1 egg
- 2 tablespoons tomato sauce
- 1 tablespoon Worcestershire sauce • Plain flour

What To Do

Mix all the above ingredients in a large bowl, except for the flour—your children will love squishing them around with their hands and it's really the best way to combine this mixture.

Help your children to shape the mixture into meatballs or patties and roll in plain flour. Cook on a well-oiled barbecue plate.

Hint!

Many other ingredients can be added to these meatballs such as chopped capsicum, corn kernels or herbs, depending on your family's likes and dislikes.

8+

BARBECUED FISH

Next time your children catch a large fish, leave it whole and help them cook it on the barbecue for all the family to enjoy. Alternatively, buy some large fish from your local fishmongers, or supermarket!

What You Need

- A large whole fish such as snapper, bream or trevally
- 1 tablespoon of butter • Dried dill • Chopped shallots
- Lemon juice • Salt, pepper • Aluminium foil

What To Do

Show the children how to clean and scale the fish, leaving the head on. Using a sharp knife, cut the fish a few times on each side.

Mix together the butter, lemon juice, shallots, dill and seasonings and place inside the fish, also smearing some into the cuts.

Wrap the fish well in greased aluminium foil and cook on the grill of your barbecue for about 20 minutes for a 1 kg (2 lb) fish.

Delicious served with chips and a salad.

BARBECUED VEGIE PARCELS

Older children will love preparing these for your next family barbecue. Best of all, they can tailor them to each family member's personal taste.

What You Need

- A variety of vegetables such as carrots, beans, peas, pumpkin, onion, corn, etc.
- Melted butter • Garlic • Seasoned salt if desired • Aluminium foil

What To Do

Chop or slice the vegetables. Help your children to arrange a variety in meal sized proportions on large squares of aluminium foil. Dot with knobs of butter and add garlic or seasoned salt if desired.

Sprinkle lightly with water and fold up the parcels so they are well wrapped in the aluminium foil.

Cook on the barbecue for 10–15 minutes.

Warning!

Unwrap carefully to avoid steam burns.

SAUCY MEATLOAF

Most children want to cook and, although it is often quicker to cook on your own, it is very important that you let them try. Think how great it will be when they are older and can take over and give you a night off! Older children will be able to do most of this recipe on their own.

What You Need

- 500 g (1 lb) minced steak • 500 g (1 lb) sausage mince (or use 1 kg minced steak if preferred) • 1 cup fresh breadcrumbs
- 2 onions, finely chopped • 2 teaspoons curry powder
- Salt and pepper • 1 egg • ½ cup milk
- ½ cup water • 1 tablespoon chopped parsley • Barbecue sauce

What To Do

Heat the oven to 180 degrees C (350 F) and grease a large loaf tin. Combine all the above ingredients in a mixing bowl except the milk and water and the barbecue sauce. When they are very well mixed, add the milk and water and mix until smooth.

Now your children can carefully spoon the mixture into the loaf tin and smooth down the top. Bake in the oven for 30 minutes. Remove and drain off any fat (parents will need to help with this part of the recipe). Invert the meat loaf onto a baking tray and cover with barbecue sauce. Bake for a further 45 minutes.

Delicious served with baked vegetables and greens. Makes enough for 6.

YUMMY PRUNE SAUSAGES

Older children will enjoy preparing these delicious sausages for the whole family and, with a little supervision, they can cook them on the barbie themselves.

What You Need
- Thick sausages—enough for the family • 250 g (8 oz) pitted prunes
- 500 g (16 oz) bacon rashers • Toothpicks

What To Do

Show your children how to prick all the sausages with a fork, then place in a large saucepan and cover with hot water. Bring them to the boil on the stove, simmer for 10 minutes then drain and cool well.

Now cut a slit in the side of each sausage and pop in three or four prunes. Carefully wrap a bacon rasher around each sausage and hold in place with one or two toothpicks.

Your children will enjoy helping barbecue the sausages until cooked. What a delicious and different family barbecue meal!

WORD PLAY

dog

log

frog

ALPHABET SPOTTING

A good game to play together when you are driving in the car,
or just a thinking game to play at home.

What You Need

- Clipboard with paper • Pen or pencil

What To Do

Before you start out on a long drive, help your children write the alphabet down the side of the paper.

As you drive along, first look for something beginning with A and write it down. Then continue with B, then C and so on. Your children can be scribes but help them with any difficult spelling. If you want to make a competition out of it, your children can write who spotted the item beside each word.

If you are playing this game at home, make it more difficult by thinking of categories. For example, animals, foods and clothing that begin with different letters of the alphabet.

BROCHURE MATCHING

A fun matching activity using junk mail.

What You Need

- Two matching advertising brochures, magazines or catalogues
- Scrapbook • Scissors • Glue

What To Do

When you next receive some advertising brochures in your mailbox, ask your neighbours if you can have theirs when they have finished reading them. Toy catalogues are great for this activity.

Cut out lots of pictures from one catalogue and paste a picture on every second page of the scrapbook, leaving the opposite page blank.

Give your children the other catalogue to look through. When they find a matching picture, they cut it out and paste it opposite its pair.

'I CAN'

Make an 'I Can' book with your children to boost their self esteem and their writing skills.

What You Need

- Paper • Stapler • Drawing and writing materials

What To Do

To encourage your children's increasing independence, talk together about things they can do on their own. These might include dressing themselves, tying their shoelaces, playing a sport, or using a knife and fork correctly. I am sure you and your children will be able to think of lots more.

Staple some pieces of paper together to make a book, or books if you have more than one child. Then your children can draw pictures of themselves on the front and write their names (don't forget to date the book so in years to come they can enjoy reading it again).

Your children draw a picture of themselves doing something they can do on their own on each page. Underneath the picture they write 'I can ...'. You will have to help them with some of the words.

Read it together. Then share it with the rest of the family and their teachers, who may like to try it with the rest of the class too. Then put it away in their special box to keep for the future.

MY BIRTHDAY BOOK

This activity provides a chance for your children to see the value of print. Making their own books will develop your children's vocabulary and counting skills.

What You Need

- Notebook or scrapbook • Writing pen
- Felt pens, coloured pencils or crayons

What To Do

Like most parents, we still talk about the joy and wonder of the day our child was born. Share this with your children and make a personalised book with them describing what happened that day.

Buy a scrapbook or notebook and help your children write the story, or you can write it for younger ones. Your children can illustrate it or perhaps even use some of the photos taken that day (or have photocopies made very cheaply at your local library).

This book is something your children will treasure, especially in the years to come when they become parents. Together you have helped create a family heirloom.

NURSERY RHYMES IN THE CAR

5+

It is still important for littlies to learn their nursery rhymes. It helps develop their memories and is also important for developing phonological awareness, skills so necessary for reading success. Older children, however, will love changing nursery rhymes and making up their own variations.

What You Need

- Long car trips

What To Do

Say an old nursery rhyme with your children as you drive along. Then make a change in the first line and see if they can make up the second rhyming line.

Little Miss Cool sat on her ...
Eating her curds and whey,
Along came a spider and sat down beside her,
And frightened Miss Cool away.

Old Mother Lantry, went to the ...

Humpty Dumpty sat on a chair ...

Neigh, neigh, black horse, have you any ...

The children will soon enjoy this game and everyone will have lots of fun thinking of unusual nursery rhyme variations.

NURSERY RHYME RHYTHMS

Listening to rhythms in nursery rhymes and songs is a great activity for your children and helps them learn about the rhythms in words and music.

What You Need

- Time

What To Do

Clap out a nursery rhyme your children know well. If they cannot identify it after a few turns, give them some clues. For example: 'It's about two children going up a hill,' or 'It's about a little girl who was frightened by something.'

When they guess correctly, they can clap one out for you to guess. A great game to play in the car on long family trips.

SONGS IN THE CAR

5+

Build on your children's interest and knowledge of rhyme by teaching them some funny rhyming songs to sing in the car on long, family trips. It certainly beats squabbling in the back seat!

What You Need

- Long car trips

What To Do

Teach the children the old Scout favourite, 'The Quarter Master's Store'.

If you don't know the tune ask around—one of your friends was probably a Girl Guide or a Boy Scout and will be sure to remember it.

There was Sue, Sue, feeling very blue in the store, in the store,
There was Sue, Sue, feeling very blue
In the Quarter Master's store.

My eyes are dim, I cannot see,
I have not brought my specs with me,
I have not brought my specs with meeeee!

Substitute your children's name and a rhyming word. For Ben it might be: there was Ben, Ben chewing on a pen. For Sam: There was Sam, Sam, eating all the ham. For Debra: There was Debra, Debra, riding on the zebra.

You will be able to think of lots of very funny rhymes for all your family and friends!

DIARIES

Diaries are a good way for your child to start a lifetime habit of writing.

What You Need

- Spiral notebook with blank page on one side and lines on the other
- Drawing and writing materials

What To Do

Keeping a diary is a great way for your children to record their activities, thoughts and feelings. Starting young, they can build an excellent writing habit for later life.

Writing in a diary each day may be too ambitious for younger children, so perhaps an entry a week may be more realistic. Encourage them to draw a picture of something that happened during the week. Then they can write the events of the week on the page opposite.

Younger non-writers can tell you what to write for them. Make sure each entry is dated at the top of the page. Remind other members of the family that diaries are private and can only be read with the owner's permission.

JOB CHART

Begin a family job chart with your children to encourage them to help out around the house. A job chart helps all the family to share tasks.

What You Need

• Large sheet of cardboard • Pens for drawing • Paper

What To Do

Talk with your children about all the chores the family needs to do to keep the home running smoothly. Make a list of them together. For example, ironing, washing, vacuuming, dusting, cleaning the bathroom, washing floors, shopping, putting shopping away, putting out garbage, cooking, setting the table, mowing the lawn, gardening, sweeping paths, cleaning the car and tidying up. I am sure you can think of lots more—it makes me exhausted just thinking of them all!

Your children can then draw a small picture of each chore on the chart.

Rule the cardboard so there is a space for each family member and room for the chores. Your children can place the chore pictures beside the family member who does them—at this stage in most families, Mum will probably be doing a lot more than the rest! If this is the case, talk to your children and the other family members about sharing more of the load.

A happy family works together.

LETTER BINGO

This game is a fun way to teach letters to your children.

What You Need

• Cardboard • Pens • Scissors

What To Do

Cut the cardboard into bingo cards and divide each card into nine squares. Randomly write alphabet letters on the bingo cards (use upper and lower case letters so your children learn both for example: 'Aa').

Cut up lots of small squares of cardboard and write the alphabet letters on them, making sure you have all the letters you have used on the bingo cards.

Give each child or family member a board and place the letter cards in a pillow case. Pull them out one at a time and hold them up for the players to see, as well as calling them out. This will help younger players. When a player has that letter on their board, they cover it with a token—buttons or small coins are ideal. The first player to cover their board calls out 'Bingo'.

For older children make it more difficult by calling out words. Then they have to place a token on the first letter of the word.

Another version of this game is that the winner also has to think of a sentence made up of words that begin with the letters on the bingo board, in sequence. The sentences are usually very funny. For instance: 'The hairy cat is lying under Dad's old brain.' Ask your children to make the sentences as unusual as possible.

MORE RHYMES IN THE CAR

Here is another rhyming activity to fill in time on long car trips. Rhymes really help to develop children's phonological awareness skills. Learning these skills is very important, for they help children to become good readers.

What You Need

- Long car trips

What To Do

Children love rhymes and enjoy making up their own, particularly if they are silly. Start them off and not only will they have lots of fun, but the trip will be over in no time. Ask them to make up rhymes about specific things they see from the car windows.

I see a car riding on a star.

There goes a dog dancing with a hog.

Once there was a train and it fell in a drain.

Everyone can take a turn and, perhaps, receive a point for each rhyme they make up successfully. A prize could be given to the first player to reach 10 points. Lollies are always popular—choose ones that are suitable for a car journey and won't make children car sick. Fruit jellies are good. So are boiled lollies, for older children.

Once they get the idea, the children will be fascinated and will love making up their own silly rhymes all the time!

RHYMING CHARADES

Listening to rhymes is an important pre-reading and reading skill. Make sure that from an early age you read your children lots of rhyming nursery rhymes, poems and books and encourage them to 'spot the rhyming words'.

What You Need

• Paper • Pen

What To Do

Help your children to think of rhyming word families. For example:

Dog, log, frog, bog
Cat, mat, fat, pat, rat
Pen, men, ten, when

Then one child can act out the words, while others try to guess what they are. See if your children can not only guess the correct answer, but write it down for spelling practice.

When they guess correctly it's their turn.

SINGING ROUNDS

Encourage your children to sing. Singing rounds in the car on long trips is a lot of fun for everyone.

What You Need

- Long car trips

What To Do

Encourage your children's musical interest and understanding by teaching them how to sing rounds.

Divide the family into two groups. If two adults are there, have an adult with each group of children. Sing a simple song that everyone knows well such as 'Home to Dinner' or the French version 'Frère Jacques'. 'Row, Row, Row Your Boat' is another easy song to sing as a round.

Group one begins and group two comes in, usually at the end of a line, or perhaps the second line.

When the first group gets to the end of the song they begin it again immediately. You can finish the round with the first group, stopping after singing the song a few times. Then the second group can stop singing on their own. Alternatively, everyone can stop singing at the end of a line together.

When you all become really proficient at rounds, tape yourselves. The whole family will be amazed at how musical they sound.

SPOT THE NUMBER PLATES

A great family game to play in the car on long trips.
It helps stop the squabbling in the back seat!

What You Need

- Bored children

What To Do

This is a really simple game and good for practising the sequence of letters in the alphabet.

Being the game by looking for the letter A on number plates, and them move on through the alphabet B, C, D and so on. The winner is the first person to spot Z.

Be warned, this game is not as easy as it sounds. It really takes a long time to spot the whole alphabet in order, especially on not-so-busy roads, and it becomes very absorbing. Recently, on a long trip with our son, he went to sleep and my husband and I played it all the way home!

DIRECTORY ASSISTANCE

Give your children practice at using a telephone directory.

What You Need

- A cassette recorder and a blank cassette
- Telephone directories

What To Do

Ask your children to pretend they are the telephone operator and, on a blank cassette, record five 'requests' for directory assistance. Use real names.

Leave enough blank tape between each request for your child 'operator' to give their name and then respond to the request. This is not only great practice at using telephone directories but also will help them become more familiar with using a cassette player.

When your children are competent at the task, record some more for them to find. Alternatively, they will enjoy looking up the names and addresses of businesses they know, or friends at school.

7+

FAMILY TREE

Help your children learn more about your family and understand family relationships by making a simple family tree together.

What You Need

- Memories (talk to Grandma and Grandpa) • Old family photos

What To Do

Get a large sheet of cardboard and print the names of your family. Add dates of births, deaths and marriages. Go back through as many generations as you can. Research the ones you don't know by asking grandparents and older relatives.

If possible, add photos to your family tree. Look for family resemblances and compare clothes and hair styles of today with those of your ancestors.

Encourage your children's awakening interest in the past by looking for historical books from the library or by visiting a historical museum together. Encourage your children to talk to their grandparents and great-grandparents about the 'olden days' so those memories are not lost.

Perhaps this activity might inspire you to organise a family reunion!

FIND THE WORD GAME

A game that tests the word skills of all the family!

What You Need

- Pencils and paper

What To Do

Find a long word and give all the players a pencil and paper. The players must try to make as many words as possible from the letters in the long word. The player who makes the most words is the winner.

A few rules: all the words must contain at least three letters; a letter may only be used more than once in a word if it is contained in the main word more than once; and it's a good idea to set a time limit for the game—perhaps ten minutes.

So, from the word CATASTROPHE you could make words such as:

TASTE, TROT, STAR, STRAP, TASTER, TOAST, PERT, TOTE, PEST, HAT and lot's more!

HANGMAN'S NOOSE

*A spelling game for older children—a great fun way
to test your children's spelling list from school.*

What You Need

- Pencil • Paper • 2 players

What To Do

Select a word your children know and draw a line for each letter in the word at the bottom of the piece of paper. Your children try to guess which letters are in the word. If they are correct, write the letter on the line. If they are wrong, add a line to the hangman's noose drawing. If you draw the whole hangman before they have guessed the word they have lost!

JUMBLED WORDS

7

Help improve your children's spelling skills in a fun way.

What You Need

- Weekly spelling list from school • Pen • Paper

What To Do

Most schools send home a weekly spelling list for children to learn. Ask your children for the list and jumble up the letters of each word. Write them down with a line beside each for the correct spelling. Your children will have lots of fun figuring them out.

Time your children each week to see if they are getting faster at working out the solutions.

SHOPPING LISTS

Encourage your children's writing skills by helping them make the shopping list before you go shopping together.

What You Need

- Paper • Pen or pencil

What To Do

Before you do your weekly grocery order, sit down with your children and write the shopping list together. Your children can do the writing—if they don't know how to spell a word, they might be able to look at packets in the pantry or advertising brochures. Or, just encourage them to have a go. Help them make the list in an organised fashion, with fruit and vegetables together, dry staples together and so on.

Take the list when you do the shopping together and they can use it.

Shopping may take a little longer, but you are helping your children learn an important life skill.

TALKING TO GRANDMA

Most children share a special bond with their grandparents. Encourage this and their interest in history by making a book about when Grandma or Grandpa was their age.

What You Need

- Paper • Stapler • Glue
- Pens for drawing and writing

What To Do

The next time you visit your parents, suggest that they talk to your children about what life was like when they were their age.

They could talk about their favourite toys and activities, things they did together as a family, games they played with their brothers and sisters, their family, their home, differences between life then and life today. Your children will be fascinated.

Encourage your children to write down what they learn. Their grandparents may have some photos they can have (or have copies made) to add to their book.

Keep the book as a special family heirloom.

ANIMAL FAMILIES

Helps older children learn both dictionary skills and animal group names.

What You Need

- Dictionary • Paper

What To Do

Do your older children know the names of animal family groups? We all know a group of birds is a flock, or a group of fish is a school, but what about some of the more unusual ones?

Write down the following words on a piece of paper,

Brace
Clouder
Drive
Gaggle
Herd
Kennel
Knot
Pace
Pride
Rather
Swarm

Your children can use their dictionary to find which animal group it describes. They can then illustrate the group.

AUTOGRAPH BOOKS

8+

Autograph books help your children's reading and writing skills.

What You Need

- Autograph books—available from toy stores, stationers etc.

What To Do

Your children will enjoy taking their autograph books to school, parties and other social occasions to collect autographs from family and friends.

Tell them that one of the rules of autograph etiquette is that you wait to read what someone has written until later; the autograph writer has to be able to get away. Of course, if they have written something rude you can always write something equally rude in their autograph book.

Some autographs I remember from my school days are:

When you see a monkey sitting in a tree,
Pull his tail and think of me!

Roses are red, violets are blue,
Honey is sweet and so are you.

I'll see you in the ocean,
I'll see you in the sea,
I'll see you in the bathtub,
Oops! Pardon me!

When you get old and cannot see,
Put on your specs and think of me!

DICTIONARY CODE

Using their dictionary will seem like fun as your children unravel this fun code.

What You Need

- A dictionary • Paper and pencil

What To Do

When your children are not around, borrow their dictionary. Begin by printing a simple message onto a piece of paper and then change the message into code. To do this you'll have to look up each word in the dictionary and then replace it with the word that immediately precedes it. For example 'What do you want for dinner tonight?' becomes (in my dictionary) 'Wharfinger djibba Yorkshire wanion fop dinky tonicity?'

Your children must use the same dictionary you have used or they will never be able to decode the message. When they are proficient at this code they can make up some messages for you to decode. They will love teaching their friends this easy code—see if their teacher can work it out too.

This activity is not only fun but will increase your children's skill with their dictionary.

LETTER STEPS

*Help your children improve their spelling and
word skills with this word-making activity.*

What You Need

- Paper • Pencils

What To Do

Do a few of these word-making activities together first. Then give your children some to try on
their own.

Choose any two words that have the same number of letters, such as MINE and SAND. The object
of the game is to change one letter at a time until the first word is changed into the second.
However, each letter change must make a new word. So, for MINE and SAND it might go like this:

MINE / MANE / SANE / SAND

or SOAP to PEAR like this:

SOAP / SOAR / SEAR / PEAR

Other words may take longer than three steps to change—try KITE to FAZE:

KITE / MITE / MATE / MAZE / FAZE

The person who can change one word to another with the least number of changes wins that
round and chooses the words for the next go. Sometimes it simply cannot be done and that round
is declared a draw.

LOOK AT WORDS

Making up anagrams (a mixed up word using the same letters) is lots of fun and a great way to improve your children's spelling ability.

What You Need

- Paper • Pencils or pens • Dictionary

What To Do

Think of some words from which to make anagrams, perhaps beginning with one of your children's names. Our son's name is ANDREW, which can become WARDEN. If the names are short, your children could make anagrams with their middle name or surname.

The weekly spelling list from school is a good place to start, too. Encourage your children to use the dictionary to check their spelling, incorporating practice in a fun game. Making up anagrams will help your children look at words in a new way.

Have a family competition to see how many words you can all make. Timing your children with the clock or the stove timer works well also.

Have them take their spelling list of anagrams to show their teacher, who might get the whole class involved.

PENPALS

8

This is a way to encourage your children to write letters and to learn about new places through a new friend.

What You Need

- Cousins who live far away, a friend from interstate met on a holiday, or friends who have moved away can all be penpals.
- Ask your school's headmaster if you can't think of anyone—schools often have sister schools in other states or countries.

What To Do

When your children start writing their letters, keep a photocopy of each one and keep the originals of the ones they receive in a large photo album. They will be fascinating to read in years to come.

Encourage your children to send lots of photos of themselves and family photographs to their penpal also. Hopefully they will return the favour—photos of themselves, their family, home, school and environment.

Happy writing!

SPELLING WORD BINGO

Hearing children's spelling can be a laborious task for parents night after night. But it is an essential one if we want our children to become competent readers and writers. Turn the spelling homework into fun by making some Spelling Word Bingo cards with the weekly spelling list.

What You Need

- Spelling homework list from school
- Cardboard • Marking pens

What To Do

Rule up a few boards divided into spaces for ten words. Choose words from the latest spelling list, as well as ones they have had to learn previously for revision. Make matching word cards with some more cardboard. The whole family may like to play also.

Call out the words and the players put a coin or button, or other marker, on the correct word. The first player to match all the words is the winner and receives a small treat. Now take away the boards, call out the words and see how well they have been learnt.

Playing Spelling Word Bingo will help your kids learn their spelling in a really fun way.

SPELLING WORD CROSSWORDS

Here's another way to make the weekly spelling homework more interesting.
Make up some crossword puzzles for your children to do!

What You Need

- You can buy a crossword book from your newsagent if necessary
and this will give you some ideas for setting the crosswords out
  - Paper • Pens • Time

What To Do

Draw up a simple crossword and think of the clues. Don't use cryptic clues for younger children. As your kids get better at crosswords, you can increase the difficulty of the clues.

Give the crossword to your children to work out. When they have finished, see if they have learnt the spelling. If they still need help, practise them together.

NUMBER GAMES

CALCULATOR FUN

Teach your younger children to be familiar and comfortable with simple calculators with fun activities like these.

What You Need

- A simple cheap calculator (if you are buying one, get one with number keys as large as possible)
- Pencils • Papers

What To Do

Show your children how to press the numbers and how to make them disappear. Show them what keys like + and – do.

Next, write some numbers on the paper for them to copy—4792, 0876, 5398, or 6748. See if they can press the numbers from 1–10, or perhaps 1–20. Call out numbers and see if they can press them correctly on the calculator—5, 8, 12, 17, and so on.

Let your children have lots of time to play with and explore their calculator in their own way. When you have things to work out with the calculator, involve them so they can see new ways to use it. Take it grocery shopping with you and show them how to work out the bargains too!

5+

DOLLAR DICE

Save all your spare 5 and 10 cent coins to play this counting game with the family.

What You Need

- A dice • Lots of 5 and 10 cent coins

What To Do

All the coins are kept in a dish, in the middle of the players. The players take it in turn to roll the dice and then take as many coins as is shown on the dice. For example—if you roll a 4 you can take 4 coins out of the dish. It is up to the players whether they take 5 or 10 cent coins.

The amounts are added up as you go and the goal of the game is to be the player who gets as close to a dollar as possible without going over the dollar! The other limit of the game is not to go over 7 rolls of the dice.

Explain to the children that while it is alright to take 10 cent coins for your first couple of rolls of the dice, it is better after that to take a mixture of 5 cent coins or you will quickly 'break' by going over the dollar.

ENVIRONMENTAL NUMBER CHART

Go for a walk around the garden or to a local park and collect lots of interesting leaves, seeds, flowers, twigs, small pebbles, grasses and other materials to make an environmental number chart with your children.

What You Need
- Large sheet of thick cardboard • Strong glue (PVA)
- Brush • Felt pens • Environmental materials

What To Do

When you come home from your walk, your children can sort out all the things you have collected into groups. Draw up a number chart together.

Help them glue on the correct number of items beside each numeral. This way they will learn to match the numeral with the number of objects.

Hang the chart in a special spot in your children's bedroom and practise counting together before they go to sleep each night.

5+

ESTIMATION

Estimating and trying to guess what is going to happen next is an important aspect of mathematics and science. Develop your children's powers of estimation by asking them questions like those listed below.

What You Need

- Building blocks • Marbles in a container • Large jug of water
- Measuring cups • Egg timer • Pencils and paper

What To Do

Use the materials above and pose questions to your children, such as:

How many blocks do you think you can build up into a tower before they will fall?
How many blocks do you think you need to lay them end to end across the doorway?
How many cups of water do you think you will need to fill up the jug?
How many marbles do you think you will need to fill a measuring cup?
How many times do you think we will have to turn the egg-timer before you have tidied your room, put away that game, or picked up those blocks?

After your children have given you their estimations, work them out together and see how close they were.

NAUGHTY THREES

A simple dice game all the family will enjoy.

What You Need

- 2 or more players • 2 dice • Paper and pencil

What To Do

Elect someone to keep the score. The game is simple and the first player to reach fifty (or any other designated number) is the winner.

Players take it in turns to throw both dice and only score when two identical numbers are thrown (two 1s, two 2s and so on). All doubles score five points, except for a pair of 6s which scores 25, and a pair of 'naughty' 3s, which wipes out the player's total score and they then have to start again!

NUMBER HUNT

*A good game to play while you cook dinner. It will
keep the children out from under your feet.*

What You Need

- Time

What To Do

Call out a number and then ask the children to find objects that represent that number from around the house. For example, a fork has four tines, so that is four; a rolling pin has two handles—two; a chair has four legs—four.

You will be amazed at how inventive they become.

FAMILY EYE-COLOUR GRAPHS

*Graphing is an important mathematical skill. Help your children make
a graph of family eye colours and learn this skill in a fun way.*

What You Need

- Paper • Coloured crayons, pencils or felt pens

What To Do

Discuss the eye colour of members of your family and extended family with your children.

Make a simple graph of eye colours—brown, hazel, green, glue and so on, and help your children discover the most common eye colours in your family.

Encourage them to take their graphs to school to show their teachers or to use for a talk.

GUESS THE DISTANCE

This is a good game to fill in those tedious times in the car on long trips.

What You Need

- Long car trip

What To Do

As you are driving in the car, have someone point out a distant landmark or object. Everyone else guesses how far away it is.

The driver checks the kilometres on the speedo and the person with the closest estimation is the winner.

LEAF GRAPHS

6+

Sorting and graphing are important mathematical skills. Activities like this will help your children gain these skills in a fun way.

What You Need

- A collection of leaves of all shapes • Paper
- Pencils • Cardboard • PVA glue

What To Do

Go for a walk in a park with your children and collect a large bag of leaves of all shapes and sizes.

Your children can sort the leaves into various categories—smooth, rough, pointed, rounded, eaten by insects, whole, etc. Help them make a simple graph by drawing the shapes of leaves they have collected. See which is the most common shape.

When they have finished, give them some cardboard and PVA glue, and they will enjoy making an interesting leaf collage with their collection of leaves.

6

MEASURING AND BALANCING

Children love working out measurements and this is a very important early numeracy skill. Turn it into a fun activity so they are learning through play.

What You Need

- A large dish of sand, dried beans, rice, or some other grain (available cheaply from produce stores)
- Balance scales • Measuring scales

What To Do

If your kitchen scales are too expensive for use by the children, visit a second hand store and buy a set for them to play with.

Give them an assortment of containers and they will love measuring and pouring, and comparing amounts. Older children will enjoy recording their findings. Pose some questions for them to solve.

If we add a cup of water to a cup of dry sand does that make it heavier?

Is a cup of rice heavier than a cup of corn?

What sort of leaf in the garden is the heaviest? Is it necessarily the biggest?

When they have had enough playing, send them into the kitchen to do some real measuring as they make a batch of pikelets (with some help from Mum or Dad) for everyone to enjoy!

ODDS AND EVENS

A fun, fast game to play with your children.

6+

What You Need

- 2 players • Paper for scoring

What To Do

You and your children must clench your right fist. Together, count to three and on three each person extends either one or two fingers. As you extend your fingers, you must take it in turns to say 'odds' or 'evens'. If the players extend one finger it is 'evens'; if one extends one and others two, it is, of course, 'odds'.

If a player guesses correctly, they score a point and have another turn at calling. When they guess wrongly, it is the other player's turn to call again. Before you begin the game, decide when it will end—perhaps the first to 20, or maybe when the clock gets to the hour.

ADDING UP HOLES

Improve your children's adding ability as well as their throwing skills with this activity.

What You Need

- Large cardboard box or piece of strong cardboard
- Craft knife • Paper to score • Felt pen • Tennis ball

What To Do

On one side of the box, or the cardboard, draw five or six different sized holes. Make the smallest one just large enough for the tennis ball to go through. Cut out the holes carefully. Above each hole write its score; the smaller the hole, the higher the score.

Prop up the cardboard or box with the holes towards the players, who then take it in turns to try to throw the ball through the holes. If a ball goes through a hole, write its score beside the player's name.

Improve your children's adding abilities by making them keep a running total. The person with the highest score after a set number of throws is the winner.

DROP DEAD

A fun and exciting family dice game.

What You Need

- 2 or more players • 5 dice • Paper and pencil

What To Do

The aim of Drop Dead is to throw the highest possible score in one turn.

The first player begins by throwing all five dice. Each time they make a throw that does not contain a 2 or a 5, they add together the total number of that throw. They then have another throw. If they do throw a 2 or a 5, they score nothing for that throw and the dice that showed a 2 or a 5 is removed from their turn. A player's turn continues until the last dice shows a 2 or a 5 and they have to 'drop dead', and the next player has their turn.

See who can make the highest score from an individual turn or add up all the scores for the highest total score.

MATCH THE TIME

Children have to learn to tell the time from analogue clocks, digital clocks and written time. Games like Match the Time will help them learn this in a fun way.

What You Need

- Analogue clock (a clock or watch with a conventional round face)
- Digital clock • Paper • Pencil

What To Do

Show your children how time is written—4.20—then show them what this looks like on an analogue and a digital clock.

Draw some circles on a piece of paper and put in the hours. These will represent the analogue clocks. Next, draw some rectangles. These will represent the digital clocks.

Next, write a list of times—4.30, 7.20, 8.48, 1.10, 8.50 and so on.

Now your children have to show these times on both the analogue and digital drawings. When they can do it with no trouble, they can set some for you to work out!

NUMBER PLATE ARITHMETIC

Do you think your children need practice with their adding up? While calculators are great, many education experts are beginning to be concerned that children cannot do simple mathematics in their heads any more. Play this game in the car and give them lots of practice while they are having fun and filling in the trip at the same time.

What You Need

- Paper • Pens or pencils • Clip boards • Car trip

What To Do

The children simply clip a piece of paper to their clipboards and begin writing down the numbers they see on other vehicles as they go along. As they write them down they do a running total. The first person to reach 100 is the winner. Of course, numbers are written down individually, for example a number plate 176 ASH would be 1 + 7 + 6 = 14 and so on.

They can challenge each other and check each other's work to see if there are any errors in the addition.

NUMBER WORDS

A fun family game to play with children to
help improve everyone's adding-up skills

What You Need

• Paper • Pencils • Hat or box

What To Do

Cut up a piece of paper into 26 squares and write a letter of the alphabet on each square. Put them all into a hat or box and mix them well.

The children number their paper down the side from 1 to 26. As each letter is pulled from the hat, it is written beside the next number. Perhaps W is pulled out first—if so, it will be 1; T second—2; M third—3, and so on.

Now everyone makes as many words as they can, trying to think of words with the highest possible numerical value. Set a time limit of 5 or 10 minutes, then add up everyone's scores and see who is the winner.

ROUND THE CLOCK

A good family game that everyone can play together.

What You Need

• A few players • 2 dice • Paper and pencil

What To Do

One player has a piece of paper and a pencil to score. Down the left-hand side, write the numbers 1–12. Then write the players' names across the top. Draw a column for each player.

Players take it in turn to throw the dice in the correct sequence 1–12. The winner is the first to complete the sequence. The scorer ticks beside the number in each player's column as they throws the correct number.

Players throw both dice each turn. For numbers 1–6, a player can score with either or both dice—for instance, a 2 and a 4 could be 2, 4 or 6. It is also possible at this stage to score twice on one turn—if a player throws a 2 and a 3, he could count both numbers.

From 7–12, however, a player will have to add together both dice. Good counting practice!

CALENDAR CALCULATIONS

Help your children learn more about using calendars with these simple problems.
Buy a calendar for their room so they can write in important dates.

What You Need

• Calendar • Paper • Pencils

What To Do

Choose the last three calendar months to work from. Set some problems for your children to solve, such as:

What date was—

> The second Friday in July?
> The first Thursday in June?
> The last day in August?
> The last Wednesday in August?
> How many schooldays are there in June?
> (Don't forget about public holidays and school holidays (if any)).
> How many weeks altogether in June and July?
> How many Saturdays altogether in June, July and August?

Problems like these will help your children understand how to use a calendar and keeping one of their own will help them keep track of important events in their life.

GALLUP POLLS

Has your household ever been phoned to take part in an information quest—a Gallup Poll? Help your children conduct one with your own family, or perhaps among their class.

What You Need
• Clipboard • Paper • Pen

What To Do

Help your children work out the questions they will ask. If it is within the family, maybe things like bedtimes, favourite meals, favourite TV programmes, favourite holiday destinations or favourite foods. School questions might include things like favourite buses, changes to the uniform, amounts of homework and so on.

When all the results are collected, help the children collate them. Perhaps you may have to make a few family changes!

HOUSEHOLD PROBLEMS

8+

Help your children work out everyday mathematics problems with examples like these. Children need to realise that mathematics is needed for real life.

What You Need

• Paper • Pencil • Your time

What To Do

Show your child examples of the sort of problems adults solve with mathematics daily. Write some of them down and see if your children can work them out (calculators are allowed).

Here are some examples:

Work out how much interest we will need to pay each year on a housing loan of $50,000 at 7.50% per annum.

We need to paint the inside of the house. The house has 10 rooms and each room needs one tin of undercoat and one tin of top coat. The undercoat will cost $35.00 per tin and the topcoat will cost $38.00 per tin. We will also need to buy a roller for $10.00 and four new brushes at $8.00 each. How much will be spending on paint and brushes?

Mum has asked you to go to the shop and buy a loaf of bread and a paper. The paper costs $0.70 and the loaf of bread is $1.85. She has given you $4.00 and said you can have the change for an iceblock. How much will you have to spend on an iceblock? Will you be able to buy your favourite, which is $1.50?

Take your children shopping with you to work out some more problems.

MAGIC NUMBER 9

8

Teach your children some of the 'magic' properties of number 9.

What You Need

- Paper • Pencil

What To Do

When your children are learning their nine times table, teach them some of the interesting properties of number 9.

Do they know that you can always tell whether a number is divisible by 9? Just add all the digits of the number together until you reduce it to one number. If that number is 9, the number you began with will be divisible by 9, no matter how big it is. Try 45 (4 + 5 = 9), then try 1214 (1 + 2 + 1 + 4 = 18; 1 + 8 = 9), or even 6,878,943 (6 + 8 + 7 + 8 + 9 + 4 + 3 = 45; 4 + 5 = 9). Let your children work out some of these for themselves.

Now try some number magic with the nine times table. To get the ten first results of the multiplication tables for 9, have them follow these simple steps.

Think of the number you want to multiply 9 by—say 7. Now subtract 1, which gives us 6. That number 6 is the first digit of your number.

Then take that number 6 from 9 and you will get the second digit of your answer—3. The answer is 63.

Of course, while all this is very interesting, remind your children that it will be a lot quicker to just learn their 9 times table off by heart!

NINE MEN'S MORRIS

An ancient game of skill to play with your older children.

What You Need

- 50 cm (20 in) square board made of wood or cardboard
- Ruler • Marking pen • Counters—9 each of a different colour

What To Do

Mark out the board as shown below, then give each player 9 counters of the same colour. The youngest player begins and players then take it in turns to put their counters on the board. They must be placed on one of the 24 circles forming the corners and line intersections on the board.

The players try to get three of their counters in a line (called 'a mill') while stopping their opponents doing the same. When a player gets three counters in a line, they can take off one of their opponent's counters, but not one already forming a line of three. That counter is then out of the game.

When all the counters are on the board, the players then take it in turns to move one counter at a time along the lines to the next unoccupied point. At this stage in the game mills can be made, broken and remade. The counters must move along straight lines, however. Each time a player makes or remakes a mill, they can remove an opponent's counter.

By the end of the game, if a player has only three counters left and they are in a mill, they must break the mill on their turn. At this stage that player is no longer restricted to the paths but can 'hop' to any point on the board.

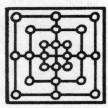

The object of the game is to capture 7 counters from the other person or create a situation where the other person cannot move.

SHOPPING CALCULATIONS

This is a good game to play with your older children. It will improve their calculator skills and teach them some shopping sense at the same time.

What You Need

• Sheets of paper • Pencils • Calculators

What To Do

Call out simple shopping equations for the children to copy down and calculate. They have to work out which items would be the cheapest for, example: 3 for $2.90 or 7 for $6.60; 3 for $64.50 or 5 for $110.00.

As each equation is solved, the first person with the correct answer gets a tick or star. The person who wins the most at the end of the game gets to choose a special treat—perhaps a family picnic destination or a special dinner menu!

8+

SPEND THE MONEY GAME

A good budgeting game to play with older children.

What You Need

- Shop catalogues

What To Do

Here is a quick mathematics activity that will help your children learn how to budget money.

Pretend with your children that you are going to totally redecorate their room. Give them a budget—perhaps $1000—and a few shop catalogues.

They have to buy the furniture, bedding, etc., from the catalogues and come in under the budget.

You could also play this game at Christmas time and give them a budget for the family Christmas shopping!

SQUARE NUMBERS

When your children have learnt all their multiplication tables, teach them this easy way to work out square roots of two digit numbers that end in 5.

What You Need

- Paper • Pencil • A calculator to check the answers

What To Do

The first step is to multiply the first digit of the number by the same digit plus one. For example, 35 squared would be 3 x 4 = 12, then simply add the number 25. The answer would be $35^2 = 1225$. Have your children check with their calculator to see if you are correct.

GAMES TO PLAY

DOTS AND DASHES

A game of skill to play with your children.

What You Need

- Two players • Pencils • Paper

What To Do

Draw lots of rows of dots on the paper first. The number of dots you draw will determine how long the game will last.

The players take it in turns to draw a line connecting one dot to another. You can draw the lines any direction but diagonally. The aim of the game is to form squares between four of the dots.

The person who draws the last line which forms a square 'owns' that square and writes their initial in it. They then have another turn.

If a single line makes two squares, that player 'owns' both squares but only gets one more turn. Help your children with the strategies of the game so they understand not to make it too easy for their opponent.

At the end, tally up the squares to see who the winner is.

MARBLE BOWLS

Make a bowling alley for your children's marbles.
A good game to play before bedtime or on wet days.

What You Need

- A box—a shoebox is ideal, or a cereal box will do
- Scissors • Paper • Marker • Marbles

What To Do

Cut arches out of the bottom of the box for the marbles to roll into. Mark the score above each arch. Then mark a spot on the floor for the players to roll from.

The players take it in turn to roll six marbles towards the box. If a marble goes through an arch, the player earns that number of points.

Appoint a score-keeper (parents are great at this) so there will be no arguments. The first player to reach a certain score—perhaps 50 or 100—is the winner or, if it's before bedtime, the player with the highest score at bedtime!

NOISY ANIMAL PAIRS

A noisy, funny game to play with a group of children.
It's an excellent party game!

What You Need

- An even number of players • Pieces of paper
- A cardboard box or container

What To Do

Divide the number of children by two and think of that many animals. They must be animals that all the players are familiar with, as the children need to know what sounds they make. Write the name of each animal on two pieces of paper. Place all the animal names in a box and the children take it in turn to draw out a name (they must keep this a secret).

Now the game begins. The children pretend to be the animal they have drawn out and they must make the noise that animal makes. At the same time, however, they must also listen to the others to find the child who is making the same noise as themselves. The first animal pair to find each other are the winners, but the game continues until everyone has found their pair.

5+

TIC-TAC-TOE

A simple game of strategy that all children love.

What You Need

- 2 players • Paper • 2 pencils

What To Do

Show your children how to draw two horizontal parallel lines crossed by two vertical parallel lines to make nine spaces in three rows.

One player draws the Xs and the other the Os. The first player to get three Xs or three Os in a row in any direction is the winner.

SIMON SAYS

*An oldie, but a goldie! And a game that creates
great hilarity among the players. Great at parties.*

What You Need

- Players • Space to play

What To Do

Explain the rules to the children. You will give them instructions, but they can only do them if they hear 'Simon says'. So, if you say 'Run on the spot', they must remain still until the command 'Simon says, run on the spot!'

Players are eliminated if they do the wrong thing. The last player in is the winner and can give the commands next time.

SLAP JACK

*A great card game to play with your children and a good
way to introduce the four suits in a pack of cards.*

What You Need

• A pack of playing cards • 2 or more players

What To Do

The aim of this game is to collect the whole fifty-two cards in the pack.

Deal out the whole pack one at a time to the players. The cards are dealt face down and the players don't look at their cards.

Take it in turns to put a card on a pile in the middle. If a Jack is turned up first player to slap the Jack takes all the cards in the middle.

Players must place the cards in the middle without looking at them first and turning the cards and slapping must be done with the same hand.

If a player slaps a card that is not a Jack, they must pay a penalty and give a card from the bottom of their pack to all the other players.

For a variation you can play 'Slap Fiver' or 'Slap Acer'.

STATUES

A good party game—or play it any time you have a group of children to keep occupied.

What You Need

- Music—a cassette or CD player or the radio

What To Do

First, the players spread out. When the music starts they begin dancing around the room. Suddenly stop the music and everyone has to 'freeze' in whatever position they were in. Watch the children carefully and the first person to move is out.

The game continues until only one person is left. That person is the winner.

BOOK BALANCING

Long ago, young ladies were encouraged to walk around with a book on their head to improve their posture. Today this is a fun game to play with a few children at a party, or just out in the back yard.

What You Need

- Books—hardcover picture books work well

What To Do

Give each player a book to balance on their head. Let them have a few minutes to practise walking before the race begins.

When the children are ready, line them up. They have to walk as quickly as possible to the finishing line with the book balanced on their head. They cannot touch the book at all with their hands. If it falls off, the player goes back to the start and begins again.

Some children find this very easy—for others it is almost impossible to do. Try it yourself and see how good your posture is!

INDOOR HOCKEY

6+

Hockey is becoming a very popular sport in our schools. Show your children how to play this simple table-top variety—great for bored kids on wet days.

What You Need

- Table • Books • Ice-cream sticks
- Paper • Masking tape

What To Do

Position thick books all around the edges of a large table, to form the sides of the hockey field. Leave a space at each end, to be the goal. Each player has a ice-cream stick for a hockey stick. To make the ball, roll a piece of paper into a ball shape and wrap masking tape around it to secure it. Let the game begin.

The players stand at each end behind their opponent's goal and take it in turn to shoot the 'ball' towards their goal. Stay around because, like most family games, an umpire is often needed!

I WENT TO THE PARK GAME

Next time the children have had enough of running around and playing in the park, sit down on a rug and play a great memory game with them.

What You Need

- A group of children

What To Do

Sit the children on the rug in a circle and begin the game by saying:

'I went to the park and I climbed a tree'.

The next player says:

'I went to the park and I played football and I climbed a tree'.

The third player says:

'I went to the park and I had a swing, and I played football and I climbed a tree'.

The game continues around the circle with everyone trying to remember all the activities.

LEAPFROG

This game is great for parties or when you have a few children over to play.

What You Need

• Space to play   • A starting and finishing line

What To Do

The players find a partner and line up. When you say 'go', one player from each pair goes forward a few paces, bends over with hands on knees and head tucked in well, and the partner runs up and puts their hands lightly on the back and leaps over.

They then repeat the same sequence with the other partner doing the leaping. This goes on until one pair is the first to cross the finishing line. To stop arguments it is a good idea to have an agreed number of jumps to do before the finishing line otherwise the jumps become very well spaced!

Leapfrog is not as easy as it sounds and it is often hilarious to watch. Make sure you have lots of cool drinks for the players at the end.

MARCO POLO

A game to play with lots of kids in the park, a backyard or even in the pool with good adult supervision.

What You Need

- Children • A safe area to play where they will not run into things with their eyes closed

What To Do

Someone is chosen to be 'it' and must close their eyes. (If you find they are cheating with this part put on a blindfold—a scarf or one of the blackout blindfolds from airlines work very well). The person who is 'it' may say 'Marco' and the other players reply 'Polo'. As he hears them, he moves towards them and they move away. When he finally catches someone, they are now 'it' and have to close their eyes and say 'Marco'.

NEIGHBOURHOOD BOARD GAME

6+

Make a Neighbourhood Board Game to play with your children.

What You Need

- Cardboard • Coloured felt pens, pencils or crayons
- Coloured containers • Dice

What To Do

Next time you go for a neighbourhood walk with your children encourage them to look at street signs, how streets intersect, parks and other unusual features of your neighbourhood. You may even like to take a small notebook with you, to jot down any ideas they have on the walk.

When you have time at home, make a Neighbourhood Board Game together on a large piece of white cardboard. Use your home as the start and another feature—perhaps a park or a corner store, or a friend's home—for the finish. Mark the route out in squares and the children will enjoy marking in features they remember from walks.

The children will have many ideas such as:

A local shop: miss a turn while you eat your iceblock; or move ahead 2 squares for picking up a paper. Mail box: throw a 5 to move after you post your letter. Crossing: move ahead two squares because you crossed at the crossing.

The whole family will enjoy playing a board game that is about your own neighbourhood.

NUMBER PLATE BINGO

A great game to play in the car on long trips.
Just needs a little preparation before the trip.

What You Need

- Paper • Pencils or pens
- Hard books or clipboards

What To Do

You need a piece of paper per child for this game. Before you leave home write the letters of the alphabet from A–Z in capital letters on a piece of paper, or have the children do it.

When they start to become restless on a long car trip, hand the pieces of paper out. The children have to cross off the letters of the alphabet as they spot them on the number plates of other vehicles. When they spot a letter they yell it out so Mum or Dad or the other players can verify it. The letters do not have to be crossed off in alphabetical order, so the game is fairly fast.

TREASURE MAPS

Help your children to make a fun treasure map, for use when they have friends over to visit. A great indoor or outdoor activity.

What You Need

- Pencils or felt pens • Paper
- A 'treasure' (a small jar of lollies makes a good one)
- Scissors • Small piece of ribbon

What To Do

Help your children to look around the house and garden, and find a suitable spot to hide a treasure. If playing this game outdoors, they may even like to put their treasure in a tin or box and bury it in a flowerbed.

Next, the children draw a map, with clues to the whereabouts of the treasure. Clues such as 'Six paces from the washing line and turn right' are good. For younger children, be sure not to make the clues too hard or they will lose interest. For older children, make the clues really cryptic.

When your children's friends arrive, they will take great delight in the treasure hunt. This is also a great game for parties. Older children in the family can design treasure maps for younger children's parties.

6+

ALLITERATIVE FUN

Next time you have a long car trip, long wait for an appointment, or time to fill in, play a game with the children that's fun but will also teach them those important phonological awareness skills so necessary for good readers.

What You Need

- Time to play together

What To Do

Make up your own alliterative sentences—alliteration is the ability to hear the first sound in words.

Freddy Fryer freaks out at football.

Billy Bloggs booted the ball.

Samantha Sly skated on Saturday.

See how many the children can think up. Encourage them to think of silly ones if possible. Soon they will all be enjoying the game and having lots of fun.

APPLE BOBBING

My son played this game recently at his friend Billy's sixth birthday party.
It was a big hit with all the children!

What You Need

- A large dish of water per child • An apple per child

What To Do

The children each kneel in front of a dish containing an apple floating in the water. An adult says 'go' and the children have to try to catch the apple in their teeth and eat it without using their hands.

A fun party game but best played on a nice warm day because all the kids get rather wet!

Warning!

Any activities that involve children and water must always be carefully supervised by an adult.

HEADS DOWN, THUMBS UP!

A great party game, or a game to play with a large group of children.

What You Need

- Chairs outside • Lots of players

What To Do

This is a nice quiet game to play at a party or a gathering of children when they are all getting too rowdy. A nice quiet classroom game too!

Three children are chosen to be 'it'. The other children sit down and close their eyes and hold out their hands with their thumbs up. Anyone spotted peeking is IMMEDIATELY OUT OF THE GAME!

The three children who are 'it' confer together quietly and decide who they are going to touch. They then each move quietly around and touch the child they have selected on the thumb.

The three 'its' return to the front and all the children are then told to open their eyes. The three children whose thumbs were touched take it in turn to name which of the 'its' they think touched them. If their guess is correct they become one of the 'its' for the next game. If they didn't guess correctly they sit down and that child stays 'it' until someone else guesses correctly.

Children need to develop strategies for this game like not touching their best friends all the time.

MOONLIGHT STARLIGHT

7+

This game still sends shivers down my spine. It was a favourite game of my sister, cousins and I when we were kids. We played it at countless family get-togethers.

What You Need
- Children • A dark night

What To Do

One child is chosen to be the 'boogie' and goes and hides in the dark. The other players count to 100 and then come out chanting 'Moonlight Starlight, boogie won't come out tonight'. Of course the 'boogie' waits until they are really close to her hiding place before she comes out and grabs a victim. This game always involves lots of screaming so warn the neighbours! The person grabbed becomes the next 'boogie' and the game continues until the adults have had enough.

NUMBER PLATE NAMES

Long trips can be tedious for everyone, especially the driver if there are ructions in the back seat. Here is another simple activity that will bring a smile to everyone's face.

What You Need
- Number plates • Bored children

What To Do

Next time you are going somewhere in the car and the children start to fidget and squabble, play this game. Spot a number plate and think of the funniest name you can for the letters on it. For example EHL might be 'Ernest Hemingwaite Longbottom' or APP might be 'Aloicious Percival Pot'.

This game is guaranteed to reduce them all to fits of giggles.

THE CHICKEN AND HAWK GAME

Another old playground favourite that is great for birthday parties or whenever you have a group of children together.

What You Need
- Children • Space to run safely
- Chalk to mark lines on the ground

What To Do

Mark out the boundaries for the game by drawing two lines about three metres apart. Choose two of the children to be the hawks and they stand in the middle of the two lines while the rest of the players, the chickens, stand behind one of the lines. When you say go the chickens must run across to the other line, trying to avoid being caught by one of the hawks. Any players who are caught join the hawks until all the children have been caught.

The last child to be caught becomes the next hawk and chooses a friend to help.

THE LISTENING GAME

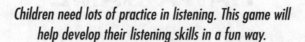

*Children need lots of practice in listening. This game will
help develop their listening skills in a fun way.*

What You Need

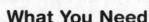

- A group of children • Space to play

What To Do

One child is chosen to stand at the front of the group facing a wall. The rest of the children stand a few metres behind.

When you signal, the children try to sneak up on the child at the front without making a sound.

If the child at the front hears any noise they turn around and point to the person who made the noise. That child has to go back to the start and begin again. While this is happening, the other children freeze until the child at the front turns to the wall again.

The winner is the first child to reach the child at the front without being heard.

COIN TOSSING

Another good game that not only improves your children's throwing skills, but also gives them counting practice.

What You Need

- Muffin tin • Pencil • Paper • Coins

What To Do

Cut out circles of paper to fit in the holes in the muffin tin. Give each hole a different number. Stand the tin against some books so it stands on an angle.

Mark a spot for the players to throw from and let them take it in turns to try to toss a coin into one of the holes in the muffin tin. Coins that land in a hole score that number of points.

Players must add up their own scores and keep a running total. The first player to reach a designated score (perhaps 100) is the winner.

GUESS WHO?

A family game to play together. It's also an ideal party game.

What You Need

- Pieces of paper • Tape or safety pins

What To Do

Before you begin the game, write the names of several famous people on the slips of paper. Choose one person to have the first turn and pin a famous name on their back. They then have to try to discover who they are by asking questions like—'Am I a female?', 'Do I star in movies?', 'Am I Australian?', 'Was I born in England?' and so on.

They can only receive 'Yes' or 'No' answers and they can only ask each person one question before they ask someone else.

At the end of the game, the player who discovered the identity of the famous person with the least number of questions is the winner.

JACKS

Jacks is a game that has been played for centuries. When I was young we called it 'knuckles' and played it with real bones!

What You Need

- Plastic or bone jacks or knuckles • Small rubber or tennis ball

What To Do

Buy your children a set of jacks from a toy shop or chain store.

This is a good game to play at school, as a set of jacks and a small ball are easily fitted in school bags. Jacks is a game of skill and can be played alone, or with friends. A smooth, level surface is needed on which to play the game.

The game begins by scattering the jacks on the playing surface with a single movement of the hand. Once the jacks are down they mustn't be moved except for the ones being played with. If playing with others, children take turns when a player misses.

The game is played like this:

1. The children throw the ball up, pick up one jack, let the ball bounce once and catch it in one hand. The jack is then moved to the other hand and this continues until all the six jacks have been picked up and are in the other hand.

2. Next, the jacks are scattered again and picked up in the same manner as before but in twos, threes, fours, fives and sixes.

Lots of fun and, like all games, the more the children practise the better they will become.

PARTNERS

An excellent ice-breaker to play at a party, or fun to play with the family.

What You Need

- An even number of players
- Pieces of card • A pencil or pen

What To Do

Put on your thinking cap and try to think of as many things that go together as you can.

Here are some to get you going:

Adam and Eve	Spaghetti and meatballs
Knife and fork	Bread and butter
Bacon and eggs	Soap and water
Hide and seek	Cup and saucer
Bat and ball	Jack and Jill
Night and day	Cats and dogs
Batman and Robin	Hansel and Gretel

I am sure you will be able to think of lots more. Write down half of each pair on one piece of card and its pair on the other. Shuffle up the cards and deal them out. Each player receives a card. The players then go round the room trying to find their partners (meeting everyone else as they go).

The first pair to find their mate are the winners, but the game continues until everyone is matched.

TRAFFIC SIGNS GAME

Here is another great spotting game to ease
the tedium of long family trips in the car.

What You Need

- A clipboard per child • Paper • Pencil

What To Do

Give the kids a clipboard each to clip their paper on in the car (inexpensive clipboards can simply be made with a bulldog clip attached to the top of a piece of very thick cardboard).

Ask the children to try to spot as many different traffic signs as they can on the trip. When one spots a sign they draw it or write down a description of it. A sign can only be spotted once in the game.

At the end of the trip or at a designated time, count up to see who has spotted the most signs.

8+

WHO IS IT?

A good game to play at a party.

What You Need

- A baby photo of each child coming to the party
(obtain them secretly from the children's parents beforehand)
- Pencils and sheets of paper

What To Do

Pin or Blu-Tack the baby photos up on a wall or a piece of board and number each one. Give each child a piece of paper with a list of all the children who are at the party.

The children then wander around looking at the photos (and probably at each other) until they have written a number beside each name.

Have a time limit on the game and then see who has the most right. Have an appropriately funny prize for this game—perhaps a big tin of baby powder or a big baby's dummy!

YO-YO FUN

Yo-yos are one of those perennial toys that surface every few years. When I was a child they were really popular. My six-year-old son considers them 'cool' so they must be back in fashion again!

What You Need

- A yo-yo

What To Do

If you think you are a bit of a yo-yo champ from way back, it might be a good idea to practise some of these tricks while the children are at school or otherwise occupied, or you may end up with egg on your face!

One basic trick is called 'the Sleeper'. Toss the yo-yo out the back of your hand with a flick of your wrist. When the yo-yo drops to the bottom of the string, try to stop it slightly and the yo-yo will spin. Jerk your hand upwards slightly and the yo-yo will come back up the string very quickly. This is a basic trick but, like all yo-yo tricks, it takes practice. In time you or your children will be able to let the yo-yo rest at the bottom for a few seconds, before it comes back up the string.

Another famous trick is called 'Walking the Dog'. First you do a 'sleeper' as hard as you can, so the yo-yo really spins at the bottom of the throw. As it is spinning, place it gently on the floor—tiles, wood or other hard floors work much better than carpet. Walk a few steps as your yo-yo spins and you'll be walking the dog. Again this takes a lot of practice even though it sounds simple!

You and your children will have lots of fun revisiting yo-yos and learning all the tricks together!

OUTDOOR ACTIVITIES

ART AT THE BEACH

When the children are tired of swimming, or need something to do at the beach when it's too cold to swim, do some beach art with them.

What You Need

- Buckets for collecting bits and pieces

What To Do

Go for a long walk on the beach with the children (don't forget the sunscreen!) and collect bits and pieces such as shells, seaweed, driftwood, stones, etc.

The children will have great fun making pictures in the sand and using their beach materials for collage.

Take some photos before you leave—and before the waves wash it all away!

5+

FLYING SAUCERS

Make some exciting Flying Saucers to fly in the backyard with the children.
See whose Flying Saucer will fly the greatest distance.

What You Need

- Paper plates • Paper cups • Scissors
- Sticky tape or masking tape • Felt pens

What To Do

Begin by helping the children cut the paper cups in half. Keep the bottom part and cut small slits along the top edge. Then bend the slits outwards, to make flaps. Put the cup with the flaps down onto the paper plate and fasten with pieces of sticky tape or masking tape. Finally, help the children cut flaps around the outside of the plate. Fold each flap alternately forwards or backwards. These flaps will help the flying saucer fly.

Your children will enjoy using felt pens to draw windows and doors on their flying saucers, or buy a can of silver spray paint and spray them silver to look really hi-tech.

Go outside at night and see if you can really spot some alien visitors (or more likely, wonderful sights such as shooting stars).

GRASS WORDS

Children of this age who are learning to read, are fascinated with words.

What You Need

• Sunny patch of garden • Grass seed • Small stick

What To Do

Your children will enjoy helping you dig the soil in the garden bed, for the funny writing.

Next, help them to write in the soil with the stick. They might like to write their name, a short sentence or even draw a simple picture.

Then they carefully sprinkle the seed in the indentations, cover it with a fine layer of soil and water it with a very fine spray.

Keep the seeds watered and in a couple of weeks the children will be able to see their writing as grass.

HOME-MADE QUOITS

We always played quoits at Nanna's house when we were children.
Help your own children make a set and improve their throwing skills.

What You Need

- Empty plastic soft drink bottle
- Stones • Metal coat hangers

What To Do

Put the stones into the soft drink bottle to stop it falling over and securely tape on the lid. To make the hoops, untwist the handle section of the coat hanger and retwist the wire to form circles (if this is too hard on the fingers, snap off the handle with wire cutters and just use the rest).

Place the bottle on the ground and mark a spot for the children to throw from. Older children will need a handicap. Each player has ten throws at a time. Keep the scores and the person who hoops the most quoits over the bottle is the winner.

Quoits is a good game to play on a picnic or family gathering—even the older members of the family will love to have a go.

HOT AND COLD

An oldie but a goldie to play with your children.

What You Need

- An object to hide • Space to play

What To Do

One child is chosen to have the first turn and closes their eyes while another child hides the object somewhere in a designated area of the garden.

When the object is hidden, the child who is 'it' walks around the garden looking for the object. When a long way from it everyone else calls out 'cold'. Getting closer to the hidden object they indicate by calling out 'warm', 'getting warmer', 'really warm', 'hot' and 'boiling'. If the child moves away let them know by saying 'getting cooler', 'really cold'.

This continues until the child finds the object and then someone else is chosen to have a turn.

POND FISHING

Make some simple fishing nets with your children and take them pond fishing.

What You Need

- Pantyhose • Strong wire (coat hanger wire doubled for strength works well)
- A piece of dowel for a handle • String or strong rubber bands • Wire cutters
- Pliers • A clear plastic jar or container • Magnifying glass

What To Do

Help the children make some nets to use for pond fishing. The pantyhose will help you catch small water creatures that would pass through the holes in regular fishing nets.

Thread the wire through the top of the pantyhose and cut off the legs about half way down. Attach the ends of the wire to the piece of dowel to form a handle and carefully twist the wire ends with the pliers, so they are safe.

Attach the jar or container to the bottom of the pantyhose net with the rubber bands or string.

Visit a local pond and see what you can catch. The children will be able to look at their catch in the jar at the bottom of the net. If they want to see the little creatures with the magnifying glass you may need to tip the water into another container to observe them carefully. Don't forget to return your 'catch' to the pond when you have finished with it. Always model care for the environment with your children.

PULLEYS

*Make a simple pulley with your children for lifting loads
and playing rescue games with their teddies or dolls.*

What You Need

- Fishing line reel or large cotton reel • Strong cord or string
- Two wire coat hangers or length of wire • Pliers and wire cutters

What To Do

Cut the wire coat hanger and, with the pliers, bend the wire through the reel. Put the cord over the reel and tie a hook made from the second coat hanger hook onto the bottom.

Your children can use the pulley over the branch of a tree, from a cubby house, or even from the verandah.

They can use it for all sorts of games such as lifting lunch up into their cubby, lifting sand tools, or even playing police rescue and lifting injured dolls or teddies.

To add to their interest, visit a building site together and watch cranes lifting their loads.

5+

SHAPE SPOTTING

*Take up shape spotting with the children when you
go for a walk and improve their geometry skills.*

What You Need

- Time

What To Do

Shape spotting certainly livens up walks and stops children getting bored and tired. Look for all the circles, rectangles, squares, triangles around you, as you walk. Look at trees, shrubs, garden beds, driveways, fences, plants, leaves, houses, buildings, street, traffic and advertising signs, vehicles, etc. People can be looked at too—their clothes, hats, shoes, pockets, purses, backpacks, etc.

Finally, look up at the sky and see how the power lines and clouds form their own interesting shapes.

This game is a lot of fun and really encourages the children to look at their world in a new way. Just be warned, it is quite addictive and once you start it is really hard to stop.

SIPHONS

Show the children a quick way to drain the wading pool or take some excess water out of the swimming pool by making a simple siphon.

What You Need

- Length of plastic tubing or some garden hose
- Funnel • Jug of water • Container of water

What To Do

To make a siphon you simply take a length of hose and push the spout of a funnel into it.

Hold the funnel up while your child pours some water into it, until a steady stream of water is coming out the other end. Then quickly take the funnel off and cover both ends of the hose with your thumbs—don't let any air in.

Immerse one end of the hose in the pool, put the other end at a slightly lower level and the water will begin to drain out, as you have made a siphon.

Explain to the children how a siphon works. The air is pressing on the surface of the water in the pool and, with the hose full of water, there's no counter air pressure in the hose, hence the water will flow out from the hose.

SMELLING TRAILS

*Set up a smelling trail in the garden for your children and
let them test how accurate their sense of smell really is.*

What You Need

• A blindfold • Foods with distinctive smells
such as onions, mint, cheese, apple, flowers,
a tissue dipped in perfume, a cake of soap, garlic, and so on

What To Do

Take it in turn to blindfold the children and give them each a turn at trying to identify a selection
of the 'smelly' things.

See who has the best sense of smell in the family.

STARGAZING

*Introduce your children to the beauty of the night sky
by seeing who can spot the first star, at sunset.*

What You Need

- A clear night sky • Time

What To Do

Young children are fascinated by the moon, stars and planets. Introduce them to the night sky with a small game at sunset. Take them outside and explain that the sun rises in one part of the sky and sets in another. Then explain that the stars are in the sky all the time, but we can only see them when the sun's light is not blocking them out.

Have your children look carefully up at the sky, as it darkens. The first one to spot a star could win a small prize, such as a lolly. The planet Venus is often very bright in the evening sky. You could explain to your children that the 'evening star' is not really a star at all, but a planet!

A great first astronomy lesson.

Warning!

It is very important that you explain to your children that they should never look at the sun or they may damage their eyes. Teach them this from a very early age.

WALKING TO SCHOOL

Today most children are driven to school or catch a bus.
Recent studies have shown, however, that children
who walk or ride bikes to school are more alert
and more focused in the classroom.

What You Need

- Time

What To Do

In light of current research, think about whether it is possible to walk your children to school or to ride with them on their bikes. If you don't have time, perhaps a neighbour or grandparent may be able to do it for you.

If none of these is possible leave home a little earlier and park a few streets from your children's school, and walk that distance with them. Gradually increase the distance and you will all benefit fitness-wise from the extra exercise.

If this is not possible try and find some time three or four times a week when you and the children can go for a walk or bike ride together. We all need regular exercise for healthy brains as well as healthy bodies!

WHEELBARROW RACES

This energetic activity is lots of fun to do and even more fun to watch.

What You Need

- At least four children

What To Do

Mark out a starting and finishing line for the wheelbarrow race. Divide the children into pairs. Each pair has to decide who is going to be the 'wheelbarrow' first and who will be the 'pusher'.

The 'wheelbarrow' gets down on his hands and his partner lifts him around the knees. Line them all up and begin the race.

Next time, swap over, so everyone has a turn at both roles.

Loads of laughs but make sure you play it on soft grass.

CHAIN TIGGY

A very funny game to play with a group of children
when there is plenty of space for running.

What You Need

- Space to run safely • Lots of kids

What To Do

One child is chosen to be 'it'. On 'go', everyone runs and the child who is 'it' tries to catch or tag another child. When a child is caught, he joins hands with the first child and they chase the others. As each child is caught they join the chase, holding hands with the others in a chain. Only the players at the end of the chain can tag another player.

This game is very, very, funny to watch and the players often fall over and get tangled up with each other as they run.

DECORATED BICYCLES

*In the holidays, or for a school fete, help your children arrange
a decorated bicycle competition. Any money they make could be
donated to their school, a favourite charity or the local children's hospital.*

What You Need

- Posters • Bikes • Decorations such as streamers,
  flowers, pinwheels, ribbons and so on

What To Do

Your children could tell all their friends about the competition and make posters to put in local shops and restaurants. You could even help them write a story and ask your local suburban paper to run it.

Arrange for everyone to bring their bikes to a park or the school fete at a designated time and ask someone else to be the judge—perhaps a teacher or a well-known local identity. Charge a couple of dollars for each bike entered, with some of the money being used to buy simple trophies and the rest to be donated to the school or charity.

Help your own children decorate their bikes by using any of the items listed above or anything else they can think of. They might like to decorate to a theme such as a Ghost Bike or a Batman Bike.

Don't forget to take lots of photos for the children to keep.

FLOWER POT RACES

I first saw this at a school fun day but, for safety purposes, they used large flat bean bags. Traditionally, however, it seems that flower pots were used.

What You Need

- A pair of flower pots per child (or bean bags, smooth bricks or flattish stones could be used)

What To Do

Each player needs two terracotta flower pots. They balance with a foot on each pot and go forward by moving the pot forwards with their hands, one pot at a time.

If they fall off or put a hand or a foot on the ground they have to go back to the beginning and start again. This game is rather hard and the children need a lot of strength in their arms to be able to play it. But it is lots of fun!

Using the monkey bars or flying foxes in your local park helps build arm strength in young children.

HOOPSCOTCH

When you children have mastered hopscotch really well,
give them a new challenge with a game of 'hoopscotch'.

What You Need

- Some colourful plastic hoops (available from chain stores or toyshops)
- Plastic milk or juice bottles • Strong masking or insulating tape

What To Do

The children will enjoy helping you half-fill the empty plastic bottles with water or sand so they won't over-balance.

Find a clear grassy area of the garden to set up the game of Hoopscotch. Place a hoop on two bottles and secure it with tape. Then place another hoop after it on more bottles and so on until you have a Hoopscotch track marked out. You can put two hoops beside each other so children jump into them with a foot in each hoop.

The rules are the same as hopscotch except the children jump instead of hop. One child begins by throwing the stone into the first hoop. They jump into the hoop, pick up the stone and throw it into the next one, and so on.

When they over-balance or their throw goes astray, the next player has a turn. When all the players have had their turn, the first player begins where their turn ended.

This game is much harder because the hoops are raised and the children have to jump high. If two-litre bottles are too high, use small plastic juice bottles to support the hoops. Or, as an alternative, use the two sizes of bottles to make the game varied and more interesting.

This is a wonderful warming-up activity for the whole family on a cold winter's day!

OUTDOOR BUILDING

A great idea when the children are bored and looking for something to do.

What You Need

- A very large box in which to store the junk (the children may like to decorate this)
- A variety of junk such as ice-cream containers, cardboard, paper, collage material, vinyl, fabric and leather off-cuts, crepe paper, cellophane, boxes such as shoe boxes and cereal boxes, soft pine off-cuts for hammering, cardboard cylinders, and anything else you can think of
- A tool box containing scissors, snips, hammer, nails, pens, pencils, glue, PVA glue, masking tape, sticky tape (these are best on tape dispensers) hole punch and perhaps a stapler

What To Do

Although the above collections sound rather extensive I have found, after years of teaching and being a Mum, that if you have junk and tools to use with it, the children are never bored and will happily create.

By keeping large boxes and hammering materials they will make different things outdoors to indoors. It is great for children to be playing outside rather than sitting in front of the television.

Large box constructions can be painted and decorated and incorporated into their pretend play as homes, castles or perhaps a space ship or floating galaxy!

PAPER PLANES

Make some simple paper planes and have a competition with your children to see how far they can fly them. If you have a house set on high ground have them fly their planes from the veranda top and watch which way the wind takes them.

What You Need

- A4 paper

What To Do

Fold a piece of A4 paper in half lengthways. Fold the top corner of the paper into the middle to form an arrow shape. Then fold it in again. Next, fold the 'wings' down on the sides to form the plane.

The wings of the plane can be closer in to make it like a high speed fighter jet, or sit further out to increase the aerobatics potential. You can staple along the body of the plane to make it stay in shape better. A paper clip attached to the nose will make it fly even faster!

POCKET MONEY

Children need to earn pocket money and to understand that we work to receive pay. There are many outdoor jobs they can do around the house, to help earn pocket money.

What You Need

- List of jobs

What To Do

Discuss some of the jobs that you need to do regularly around your home with your children. They can help list them for writing practice.

Jobs might include weeding or digging the garden, emptying the kitchen compost container daily into the compost bin, turning the compost in the bin, raking the lawn after mowing, hosing, sweeping paths, and so on.

Decide who would like to do which jobs and make a roster. Children will gain confidence and a sense of responsibility if they have their own special chores, and will learn that everyone in a family has to help—not just Mum and Dad.

Make some lists for the fridge door or noticeboard and the children can tick them off when they have completed their allocated chores. This is good for their memory and also a literacy experience.

POGO STICKS

Another blast from the past that your children will love!

What You Need

- A pogo stick • Space to jump

What To Do

As a child I always wanted a pogo stick! Like many toys, they went out of fashion but are now back in the toy stores. So are scooters, by the way, and our son loves his!

Consider a pogo stick as a birthday or Christmas gift. Your children will have lots of fun jumping around on them and they will help develop their balance and coordination.

Have a go yourself! See if you can still master the skill.

SANDHILL SLIDING

If you live near the beach your children will love sliding down high sandhills on cardboard shapes. If you don't live near the beach, find a grassy slope and they will enjoy sliding down that, instead.

What You Need

- A steep slope to slide down safely
- Cardboard shapes to slide on

What To Do

Many parks are built with high grassy mounds for children to slide down, or to ride bikes or skateboards down safely. If you live near the beach, high sand dunes are great to slide down too.

Visit your local electrical store—they usually have a supply of large cardboard boxes. Flatten a couple out and take them home. Then the children can help you cut the cardboard into small shapes for sliding on.

Take them to a park with grassy mounds or to the beach with sandhills and let them enjoy themselves having races down the slopes. Let your hair down and have a go too!

SHADOW TIGGY

A fun variation on the old chasey game.

What You Need

- Two or more children • Lots of space to run

What To Do

One player is 'it' and he waits and counts to ten while the other players scatter as far away as they can run.

The player who is 'it' chases them and tries to stand on their shadows. When someone is caught they join the player who is 'it' to help chase all the others.

The last player to be caught is 'it' for the next game.

SKIPPING RHYMES

As your children grow older and become more proficient skippers, teach them some longer skipping rhymes.

What You Need

- A long rope of medium thickness (available from hardware stores)

What To Do

Turn the rope and chant the rhymes as your children skip.

Jelly on a plate, jelly on a plate	(child skips in time)
Goes wibbly wobbly, wibbly, wobbly	(child skips from side to side)
Jelly on a plate.	

Then:

Sausages in a pan, sausages in a pan	(child skips in time)
Turn them around, turn them around	(child turns around as he skips)
Sausages in a pan.	

Or:

Cowboy Joe from Mexico	(child runs in and begins skipping)
Riding on his pony-o	(child pretends to ride a pony as they skip)
Hands up	(child puts hands up in the air as they skip)
Stick 'em up!	(child pretends to shoot with a gun)
Drop your guns and pick 'em up!	(child pretends to drop the gun and touches the ground to pick it up)
And off you go!	(child runs out)

SOME MORE SKIPPING ACTIVITIES

6+

Here is another to teach the children.

What You Need

- A long rope of medium thickness
  (available from hardware stores)

What To Do

Turn the rope for the children and chant the rhymes as they skip.

Teddy bear teddy bear turn around	(children turn as they skip)
Teddy bear teddy bear touch the ground	(children touch the ground while skipping)
Teddy bear teddy bear turn off the light	(pretend to turn off the light)
Teddy bear teddy bear say goodnight!	(children run out)

Or:

Blue bells, cockle shells, eevy ivy	(rope is swung from side to side like a wave and children jump over it)
Over	(normal skipping resumes)

Dutch skipping is fun for really advanced skippers. For this you need two ropes which are swung in opposite directions toward the middle. Each skipper has to jump over both the ropes. This needs quite a deal of co-ordination but is great fun to try!

TUG OF WAR

A Tug of War at family picnics or birthday parties is always great fun.

What You Need

- A long, strong rope • Willing participants

What To Do

Arrange the participants evenly on either side of the rope. Put the smallest pullers closest to the middle and the larger children and adults at the ends of the rope.

Mark a spot on the ground in the middle. The aim of the game is for one team to pull the other over the mark on the ground.

Someone yells 'Go!' and everyone starts pulling as hard as they can. Lots of fun and you will probably all have sore muscles the next day!

BAIT FISHING

*If your family enjoys fishing, it is fun and much cheaper
to teach the children how to catch their own bait.*

What You Need

- A bait net

What To Do

Not all jurisdictions allow the use of bait nets, so check before you buy one.

We have found that using a small piece of burley (bread soaked in some fish oil) works brilliantly and attracts small fish. Have a child hold each corner on the large bait net. Two wade out into the water and stand still and quiet. Sprinkle the burley in the centre of the net and wait for the small fish to come. Then the children in the water wade in with the net lifting it to catch the bait. You can also buy bait dillies which can be baited with fish or pieces of meat and left in the water until some bait fish swim in and are caught.

If a bait net is not allowed where you live, the children can also have heaps of fun with individual nets. Buy or make nets with fine mesh and long handles, similar to butterfly nets. Then sprinkle some burley on top of the water and the children wait for the bait fish to come, and try to scoop them up with their nets.

Keep the bait you catch in a bucket of salt water and use it to catch some big 'uns.

237

BUILDING BOATS

Do some brainstorming with the children to see if they can think of different ways to build some boats to sail across the swimming or wading pool. The world is changing rapidly and our children will need to be divergent, creative and persistent thinkers to cope with changes. We need to challenge and extend our children's thinking skills constantly, and to encourage their initiative and persistence to finish tasks.

What You Need

- Assortment of plastic containers • Plastic soft drink and juice bottles
- Metal and polystyrene trays • Drinking straws • Plasticine or Blu-Tack
- Small pieces of soft wood • Paper • Thin dowel or bamboo garden stakes
- Hammer and nails • Masking or insulating tape • Scissors

What To Do

Challenge the kids to see who can make the best boat to sail across the pool without sinking.

Don't forget to take some photos of the finished flotilla to keep for posterity.

CAMERAS

Cameras make great gifts for children to record the important events in their lives.

What You Need

• An easy-to-use camera • Film • Photo album

What To Do

Recently I bought my son a small camera of his own at our local post office. It only cost a few dollars and he is really enjoying taking his own shots. Another option is to buy a disposable camera with the film included. They are great for a child to take on holidays, a school camp or for a special excursion. Again, they are very easy to use.

We made a few rules with our son about his camera:

We will buy the film but he has to pay for the developing from his pocket money
We have taught him how to hold the camera still and looked at his photos to help him learn
how to frame and choose good shots
He is responsible for putting his photos in his own album

Older children will also be able to write down their own stories about their photos. You will have to write down the stories for younger children.

Encourage your children to take their cameras along to important evens such as a school sports day or other notable event at school, a special family outing, or a club sports game, so they can record all the wonderful happenings in their lives.

CAMPING OUT AT HOME

Buy a tent for the children to use for camping out in the backyard.

What You Need

• A tent • Sleeping bags • Torches

What To Do

Children love going camping, but it is not always possible. Let them camp in the backyard and they can have a chance to experience the fun of sleeping out under the stars without even leaving home.

Tents make a great present for children as they can put them up inside and outside for cubbies, as well as using them for the real thing.

Plan a barbecue or a picnic tea that you can have in the garden with the children. If it is possible, make a small campfire, but supervise it well. Cook some toast to have with honey and hot drinks for supper and don't forget the toasted marshmallows.

Have a game of 'Moonlight Starlight' or tell ghost stories around the camp fire.

When it's bedtime, snuggle down in your sleeping bag with the children and enjoy a night camping out in your own backyard!

CLEAN-UP DAY

*Make it a family commitment to encourage a love
and care for the environment in your children.*

7+

What You Need

• Old clothes • Strong gloves • Bags for rubbish

What To Do

Choose somewhere local that you believe needs a good clean-up and work there.

Unfortunately, many people still leave rubbish wherever they go. We really need to educate our children that this behaviour is not acceptable. We must emphasise that all rubbish should be disposed of in bins provided for that purpose or, if no bins are available, the rubbish should be taken home and disposed of thoughtfully there.

Make sure the children are dressed appropriately in old clothes, shoes, and strong gloves. Then, as a family, you can do your part in keeping our planet clean of rubbish.

7+

FISHING

*Encouraging your children to fish is
introducing them to a great, relaxing sport.*

What You Need

• Bait • Fishing lines and tackle

What To Do

Fishing need not be an expensive sport. Fishing rods and reels make great birthday and Christmas presents, but a hand line or fishing line strung on a bottle works just as well.

Visit your local bait and tackle shop and ask for some advice. They will be happy to help and let you know about local conditions and the best bait to use.

Remember that fishing takes patience and if your children are not endowed with that virtue, maybe fishing is not for them. Also, remember that fish bite best at sunrise and dusk, so you may have to rise a little earlier than usual. However, it's worth it when the children really catch a fish and have the pleasure of eating their own cooked fish for dinner!

FISHING NET FUN

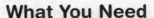

A simple home-made fishing net will provide hours of fun and sport for your children. You can use them for bait fishing or children can play with them while you are using your fishing rod.

What You Need

- A wire coat hanger • A pair of wire cutters
- Some fine but strong mosquito netting or tulle
- Needle and thread • Thin rope or strong cord
- Bait such as fish or meat

What To Do

Bend out the coat hanger to make a circle and clip off the handle section with the wire cutters. Cut out a large circle from the netting. If it is not very thick, use two layers for extra strength. Stitch the netting onto the circle of wire.

Join two pieces of rope across the top to form a cross and tie them onto the circle of wire. Attach a long piece of rope to the middle of the cross with which to pull the net up.

Place some bait in the net and the children carefully lower it into the water and wait until some small fish have entered the net and are nibbling on the bait.

FOOTPRINT CASTS

Go for a walk and find some interesting animal footprints with your children. They will have fun making permanent records of them.

What You Need

- Animal or people footprints • Small spade
- Cardboard boxes • Plaster of Paris or casting plaster

What To Do

Check in your garden, at the park or on the beach for interesting footprints. Dig up the prints with a small spade, taking enough dirt to stop it falling apart (this activity works best when there has been some rain and the ground is nice and moist). Carefully place the footprint inside a box and take it home.

At home, help the children mix up some plaster, following the directions carefully—it's important not to tip any excess plaster down drains as it may clog them up.

Pour the liquid plaster carefully into the footprint and smooth off the top with an old knife. Leave it until it is dry and hard. Brush off the dirt and you should have an exact replica of the footprint.

The children may enjoy painting their interesting footprints.

HULA HOOP

Hula hoops are great fun and also a terrific way to whittle away the waistline.

What You Need

- Hula hoop—available from sports shops, toy shops or chain stores

What To Do

If you were the Hula Hoop Queen at school in your younger days, buy a hoop for the children and see if you can still swing those hips like you did years ago.

The children might like to try using the hoop on their legs, arms, around their knees and even around their necks, as well as their waist.

See who can keep the hula hoop going for the longest time. I'll bet it won't be Mum or Dad!

7

KITES

*All children love flying kites. If your children don't have
a kite why don't you try making one with them.*

What You Need

- Plastic or a plastic bin liner • 2 thin bamboo canes
- Acrylic paints or permanent pens • Ball of string
- A short piece of dowel for the handle • Craft knife
- Paint brushes • Insulating tape • Hole punch

What To Do

Start with a piece of plastic 50 cm by 50 cm (20 in by 20 in). Help the children measure and cut out a kite shape from this. Fold each corner of the kite over and punch a hole through the double thickness. Stick strips of insulating tape in the centre of the kite—11cm (4.5 in) from the top and 7cm (3 in) from the bottom. Use a craft knife to help the children cut very small slits through these reinforced sections.

The children can now decorate their kite. When it's dry they can cut some more strips of plastic to attach to the bottom for a tail. Push one of the thin bamboo sticks through the hole in the top of the kite. Tape the stick in place with insulating tape and then do the same at the bottom. Push the second bamboo stick through the side holes of the kite and again stick in place with the insulating tape. Make sure the plastic is as taut as possible.

To attach the string, thread a metre long piece through the slits you cut earlier and turn the kite over and tie a small loop in the string. Pull it tight and the loop should be over the top slit. Tie one of the ends of the ball of string onto this loop and wrap the rest of the string around a short ruler, a short length of dowel or piece of strong cardboard. Now the kite is ready to try on a windy day.

PLANT SURVEY

7+

Teach your children about native and non-native plants. A great learning activity that the whole family can take part in.

What You Need

- Books on plant identification from your local library
- Pencils and paper • Camera

What To Do

First, go to the local library with your children and borrow some plant identification books. Explain to them that some plants are native and others originally came from other countries.

Then, take a trip to the local park or Botanic Gardens with your children and try to identify some of the plants there. You could even take the books with you, to help. The children will be fascinated as they learn the histories of different plants and where they first grew.

You could even let the children use a camera to photograph plants they are interested in, but cannot identify. Then they can use the photos to identify the plants another day. Fun and informative for everyone!

SAND MODELLING

Take the children to the beach in winter for a great sand modelling competition.

What You Need
• Sand at the beach • A few children

What To Do

Meet some friends and their children at the beach on a winter's day and organise a sand-modelling competition for the children. If you decide to have inexpensive prizes, make sure there is something for everyone.

Think of some different categories such as:

The best cartoon character
The best self portrait
The best decorated sand castle
The best sea creature

While the children are busy creating, mark out an area and bury a few 'treasures' such as well-wrapped sweets or simply cheap novelties. Later they will enjoy having a treasure hunt in the marked-out area.

When they are all exhausted, have a great picnic together. Everyone will be starved after all their hard work! Don't forget the camera so you can capture those works of art for posterity.

SCAVENGER HUNTS

*Go for a bush walk or a beach walk with the
children and send them on a Scavenger Hunt.*

What You Need

- Lists written before you leave • Treasure bags

What To Do

Go for a walk through a park, beach or forest and ask the children to use their eyes to think
creatively. Give them a list each and a bag to collect their items in.

Remind them to only collect things they can return safely and without damage.

Things on the list may include:

a flower
a chewed leaf (not by them)
something prickly
something soft
something smooth
something that is a covering
a camouflaged animal or insect
something that reminds them of themselves
something that is dead
something from an animal

Sit down and let them be the scavengers. Share the contents of everyone's bags together and
discuss the interesting items. Remind the children to return them before you leave.

TORCH TIGGY

A fun family game to play at night in the backyard or on the beach.

What You Need

Dark • Lots of players • A torch

What To Do

One player is 'it' and has the torch. They count to ten while all the other players scatter as fast as they can. The player who is 'it' tries to catch one of the other players with a beam from the torch. When they have caught someone, they yell their name and that person becomes 'it' for the next game.

CARING FOR OTHERS

Children are generally moved by the plight of those in need. We should model caring and respect for others, and empathy for inequities and unfairness.

What You Need

- Time with your child

What To Do

Talk to your children about ways you could assist others less fortunate in the community.

You may be able to:

Collect with your children for a charity such as Blue Nurses, Cancer Fund or the Salvation Army.
Take toys, clothes and other items no longer used to a charity store.
Use pocket money near Christmas time to buy toys for children who would otherwise go without.
As a family, sponsor a child in a third world country.
Care for an aged person living nearby, helping with shopping, gardening or housework.
Volunteer to do a service such as 'Meals on Wheels' in the school holidays together.

Your children will feel a sense of satisfaction by helping others and will hopefully grow into caring, thoughtful and empathetic adults.

FIND THE BELL

Listening games like this help children develop good listening habits in a fun play way.

What You Need

- Blindfolds (if you know a frequent airline traveller, ask them to collect some sleep-masks for you)
- A bell • Play to open space to play the game

What To Do

Blindfold all the players except one. That person is 'it' and carries the bell. The bell must be rung all the time, while the others try to catch the player ringing it. The player who is 'it' must work very hard to stay out of the way of the others.

Whoever tags that player has the next turn at ringing the bell.

GARAGE SALES

8+

*Help the kids organise a garage sale and unload lots of junk,
making some money at the same time.*

What You Need

- Time • An ad in your local newspaper
- Cardboard for signs

What To Do

When the kids want something special that you can't afford, suggest they help you organise a Garage Sale. Then they can sell lots of old toys they no longer play with and buy it themselves.

If your house is like ours it will take a few weekends (or some holiday time) to sort out all the cupboards. Tidy each cupboard and put into boxes any items, clothes, linen, books, magazines, toys, and tools you no longer use. You will be amazed what you unearth!

Our local newspaper even sells a Garage Sale kit with information, posters and so on. Perhaps yours does too. If not, it is important to place an advertisement in your local paper for the day of the sale. Composing the ad is good literacy practice for the children. They will also enjoy helping make some large signs to put up in your local area and perhaps a few at local shops.

Make sure you organise plenty of change the day before and money belts for family members to wear. Think of the numeracy skills the children will gain as they work out change, and the social skills they'll need for all the bargaining customers!

Go to bed very, very, early the night before your Garage Sale because people begin arriving at the crack of dawn! At the end of the day you will be exhausted, but the children will be wealthy enough to buy their own special toy and you will have a much tidier home!

GEM COLLECTING

Visit a local gem field or plan a family fossicking holiday. The kids will have a terrific time, even if you don't have any big finds.

What You Need

- See a travel agent or do some investigating of your own to see where you could go
- Camping equipment • Maps of the area you are travelling to

What To Do

There are many areas you can visit to try your hand at fossicking; places where you can collect interesting semi-precious stones, thunder eggs and other minerals, as well as places to fossick for precious stones.

Families who do this usually get hooked, and fossicking becomes a way of life. Start a new hobby for your family and take up fossicking. Who knows, one of the children may be a geologist one day or you may make a huge find!

HOSPITAL TIGGY

A fun chasing game to play with a group of children.

What You Need

- Lots of children • Space to run safely

What To Do

One player becomes 'it' and has to try and tag the other children. When they catch someone, the person tagged has to hold the spot on their body where they were tagged and also becomes 'it'.

The children get better at this game and try to tag people in places that make it very, very, difficult to hold while running, such as feet!

MAKE A BIRD FEEDER

During winter when food is scarce, make a
bird feeder to attract birds to your garden.

What You Need

- 1 piece of marine ply or craftwood 40 cm (15 in) square
- 4 strips of wood 37 cm (14 in) long • Small nails
- Hammer • Paint or Estapol • Wild bird seed

What To Do

Help your children nail the strips of wood around the edges of the square piece of wood. Leave a small space at each corner so water can drain away when it rains.

Paint or Estapol the feeder, to protect the wood.

Wedge the bird feeder firmly into a branch of a tree or fix it to the top of a tall post. Position the feeder in a leafy and protected part of the garden.

Keep a supply of wild bird seed on the feeder and the birds will soon find it. Make sure there is a birdbath or other safe supply of fresh water close by also.

MESSAGE ON THE BEACH

8+

Next time you are at the beach help the children leave a message behind.

What You Need

- Sticks or natural materials

What To Do

Brainstorm with the kids to decide what they want to write and how they want to do it. They could use large pieces of driftwood to write giant letters on the beach or use natural materials such as shells, pebbles, seaweed, and driftwood, to make the words.

Perhaps they could make the words large enough to be seen by aeroplanes or, if they use their imagination, by alien spacecraft. Well ... you never know!

NEIGHBOURHOOD WATCH

*Go for a walk with the children and see if they can
spot all the items in this neighbourhood game.*

What You Need

- Paper • Pencils

What To Do

Before you go for your walk, do some brainstorming with the children about things they may be
able to spot in the neighbourhood.

They may see:

A dog	A blue roof
A cat	A basketball hoop
A pet bird in a cage	A caravan
A flag pole	A set of swings
A white gate	A swimming pool
A brick fenceA sprinkler	A sprinkler
A metal letter box	

The children can write out their own copy of the list and, as you walk, the first person to spot an
item on the list crosses it off. The first child to cross off all the items on the list is the winner and
gets to choose their favourite meal for dinner!

RED ROVER

8

This is a great game to play with a large group of children.

What You Need

- Time • Space to run safely

What To Do

Divide the children into two groups and line the groups up facing each other, standing about 5 metres apart. Each group holds hands tightly.

One child is chosen from each group to be the 'caller'.

The caller from one side calls 'Red Rover, Red Rover, send (Tom) . . . right over'. If Tom's name has been called he must run to the opposite side and try to break through the line. He will try to choose what he thinks will be a weak link in the line. If he manages to break through, he returns to his team and chooses a child from the opposing team to go across with him. If he can't break through in a few minutes he joins the opposing team.

The caller from the other team then has a turn at calling someone across and the game continues until one team has all the players or until the end of the designated playing time.

Supervise this game carefully as it can become a bit rough!

8+

STONE SKIPPING

Teach your children this age-old pastime.

What You Need

- Flat stones • Still water

What To Do

My father taught me to skip stones across water, just as his father probably taught him.

The first thing to do is to pick out stones that will skip well. The best skipping stones are thin and flat, as they really can bounce across the water.

Next, show your children the correct technique. Demonstrate how to hold their throwing hand in front of them so that their thumb and forefinger forms a letter 'c'. The stone should be sitting in the grip with the flat side parallel to the ground.

Throwing should be done with a sidearm movement, away from the body, similar to the action needed to throw a frisbee or quoit. At the last second, before releasing the stone, show them how to give a flick of a wrist so the stone takes off spinning.

When your children have perfected the technique, have competitions to see who can make their stone do the most skips or who can skip a stone right across the watercourse!

SUNDIALS

Children are fascinated by the sun and the passing of time.
Help your children make their own sundial for the garden.

What You Need

- A piece of marine ply or craftwood about 30 cm (12 in) square
- A piece of marine ply or craftwood cut to a right-angled triangle
- PVA glue • Large pot or terracotta pipe • Permanent pens or paint

What To Do

Ask your local hardware store to cut the wood to the shapes and sizes you need for this project, if you don't have the tools and expertise to do it at home. Help your children stand the triangle up and glue it from the centre of the square to a position along the midpoint of one side.

Position the sundial on the large pot or on the pipe set into the ground, and place it in a spot in the garden where it will receive full sun.

Get up with the children when the sun rises and mark the point where the shadow falls at the hour. An hour from that time mark the next hour and so on, throughout the day.

It will be interesting for the children to observe if the sundial shows the same hours during different parts of the year, or when it is raining. Help them write up what they did as a school project and take some photos of the process of making and using the sundial, to add to the project.

TYRE PRESSURE CHECKS

Show your children how to check the pressure in your vehicle's tyres.

What You Need

- Tyre gauge (available from garages and auto accessories stores) • Cold tyres

What To Do

Last year when I attended a Defensive Driving Course I was surprised to learn how important it is to have the correct amount of air in my vehicle's tyres. Did you know that, apart from less efficient braking and cornering, under-inflated tyres can reduce your mileage and cause your tyres to wear faster?

Your children can help by prompting you to check your tyre pressure regularly or, if you buy a tyre gauge, teach them how to check the pressure for you at home when the tyres are cool.

Show your children how to remove the valve cap, fit the gauge over the cap and press. In time, they will be able to correctly read off the number and compare with the recommended pressure for your vehicle. Then it's off to the garage if the tyres are too low.

With the children on the job there is no excuse for not getting the maximum wear out of your tyres, as well as being energy-conscious and saving fuel. In addition, think how experienced they'll be at tyre pressure checking by the time they are drivers, too!

WASHING THE DOG

A great way for the children to earn some pocket money!

What You Need

- Warm water • Dog or person shampoo • A soft brush
- A few drops of eucalyptus oil • A towel

What To Do

Make washing the dog a regular pocket money activity for your children. In summer, it is best if they wash the dog in their bathers and in winter, in their oldest clothes. They will probably end up wetter than, or certainly as wet as, the dog!

I like to soap our dog all over and then give him a good scrub (especially around the tail) with a soft scrubbing brush. I always add a few drops of eucalyptus oil to the rinse water as this smells very nice and helps repel fleas. Our dog likes to be towelled off but smaller dogs could be dried with the hair drier.

What a great way for the children to earn their pocket money and have a clean dog at the same time.

WILD BIRD SEED CAKE

*During winter when food is scarce, help the children make
some wild bird seed cakes to attract birds to your garden.*

What You Need

- Wild bird seed • Sunflower seeds • Pumpkin seeds • Oats
- Chopped nuts • Dried bread • Lard or other solid fat
- Small empty margarine or yoghurt containers
- Strong twigs • String

What To Do

The children will enjoy helping chop up the nuts and mixing all the other dried ingredients for the bird cake. Melt the lard or other solid fat in a saucepan over a low heat. When it is completely melted, mix it well with the dry seed mix.

Spoon the mixture into the yoghurt or margarine containers. Push a twig into the middle of each container and leave until it has set completely. Take the cakes out of the containers and roll in some more wild bird seed.

Hang in trees in your garden with some string. Place them near branches where the birds can perch safely.

EXPLORING THE ENVIRONMENT

ANT FARMS

Children are fascinated by small creatures like ants and spiders. Help your children learn more about ants by building an Ant Farm together.

What You Need

- Large plastic soft drink bottle
- Drinking glass • Garden soil • Craft knife

What To Do

Cut the soft drink bottle in half with a craft knife. Discard the top section. Find a drinking glass that will fit inside, leaving a space about 4 cm (1.5 in) wide between the glass and the plastic bottle (it should not be any wider or you will not be able to see the ants and their tunnels).

Carefully spoon in garden soil to fill in the spaces. Add some ants from the garden and cover the top with some flyscreen so they cannot escape. Add a very small amount of cake, sugar or honey-soaked bread every few days.

Your children will be enthralled by the ants' busy lives and by their tunnelling skills.

Although you may consider ants in the garden to be pests (we do when they dig up the sand between the pavers!), it is best to teach your children to have respect for animal life by returning the ants to their natural habitat after a few days.

BARREL GARDENS

Children love to have their own 'patch' in the garden but, if space is a problem, why not try a barrel garden? Whole or half-barrels are available at garden centres, nurseries or perhaps your local distillery or winery.

What You Need

- A large barrel, or half-barrel
- Good quality potting mix
- Nasturtium seedlings or seeds

What To Do

Position the barrel where you want it to be before you begin, as it will probably be too heavy to move when it's full of soil. Most annuals need full to nearly full sun so check this before positioning your barrel.

Your children will enjoy helping to fill the barrel with the potting mix—remember that inhaling potting mix dust has led to health problems, so make sure it's kept moist. When the barrel is almost filled to the top with the potting mix, give it a good soaking so the soil is ready for planting.

Nasturtiums look great because they are so colourful and their weeping habit suits a barrel, but your children can choose any seedlings they like. If you do choose to grow nasturtiums in your barrel garden the flowers can be picked, washed and added to salads for a tasty and colourful touch. They taste great in sandwiches too!

BIRD NESTS

Children are always amazed and fascinated by bird nests.
Help them learn more about our feathered friends.

What You Need

- Time • Pencils • Paper
- Books on birds from local library

What To Do

Bird nests can be found in the garden at most times of the year—you just need to know where to look! Dense bushes and under the house and garage eaves are favourite nesting places.

Take your children to the library and borrow some books on bird watching. Show them pictures of nests and explain how birds build the nests twig by twig. Children will be amazed to learn that birds like magpies and ravens often use interesting bits of rubbish they find lying around, like plastic bags, to incorporate into their nests.

Now take your children outside on a bird nest hunt. Look carefully in bushes in the garden, or at your local park. If it is autumn or winter time, you are sure to find an old abandoned nest for the children to look at. In springtime, explain to the children that they must not touch the nests or disturb any nesting birds. If you are very lucky, you may find a nest with eggs. This will be a great thrill for the children.

After the bird nest hunt, your children might like to draw the nests they saw and the types of birds they think they might belong to.

BUTTERFLY HUNT

Butterfly collecting was a popular hobby in years gone by. Teach your children to be more environmentally friendly by capturing butterflies on film, instead of in a net!

What You Need

- Camera • Scrapbook • Glue • Pencils
- Books on butterflies from local library • Time

What To Do

Borrow some books on butterflies from your local library and read them with your children. Identify which species you are likely to find in your area, then take the camera out into the garden or down to your local park on a bright, sunny day.

The children will have hours of fun spotting and trying to identify butterflies. Help them to take photos of these pretty creatures. After the photos have been developed, your children can stick them in a scrapbook. Write the names of the butterflies beneath the photos, for younger children. Older children can do this themselves.

5+

CATERPILLAR COLLECTIONS

During the year many different types of caterpillars live in our gardens. Your children will enjoy observing and watching them change during their life cycle.

What You Need

- An ice-cream container • Fine flyscreen mesh
- Caterpillars and some of the leaves on which they were found

What To Do

When the children find a caterpillar in the garden, an ice-cream container with the fine mesh across the top makes an ideal home. Place leaves on which the caterpillar was found in the container and replace daily with fresh ones. Sprinkle a few drops of water on the leaves each morning.

When the caterpillar is in its cocoon, put it in a safe place where the children can see it but not touch. A chrysalis in a cocoon doesn't like being bumped. If the children are lucky they will be able to see the butterfly or moth emerge from the cocoon. Release the butterfly to live its brief life in your garden.

Different caterpillars live in your garden during the year; perhaps the children might like to keep a diary of which ones they see (and keep the diary with their butterfly scrapbook!).

Visit your local nursery to find out which butterfly attracting plants grow well in your area and the children will enjoy helping you plant some in your garden to encourage a variety of butterflies to your backyard.

COLD FLIES

5+

Help your children learn more about living things
with this simple science experiment.

What You Need

- A bottle with a metal screw-on lid
- A hammer and nail • Flies

What To Do

Punch some holes in the lid with the hammer. Then catch a fly and put it in the bottle.

Next, put the bottle in the refrigerator for a few minutes. Take it out and show your children what has happened to the fly. Explain to your children that the cold has slowed down the fly's metabolism (the energy producing process of living things) so the fly cannot move as quickly as before.

Discuss with your child or help them read books about animals that hibernate in cold weather. When the fly has warmed up, watch it return to normal and then let it go.

FRUIT STICKERS

Children love to collect things and collecting fruit stickers is a fun, cheap way to begin being a 'collector'! Your children will gain valuable mathematics concepts in a fun way as they sort, classify and order their fruit stickers. They will also learn a lot about fruit.

What You Need

- Scrap book • Stickers from fruit

What To Do

Most fruit today comes with small stickers on it telling us what variety it is and sometimes, where it comes from. Help your children save the stickers from their apples, bananas, oranges, mandarins and other fruit.

They can stick them in a scrap book under the various varieties of fruit, thus learning about the different varieties of fruit and what they taste like.

For example: Apples—Delicious, Granny Smith, Golden Delicious, Hi Early, Jonathans.

If the fruit is marked where it comes from, help your children trace a large map of your country for the front of their scrapbook and they can put some of the stickers on the places where the fruit is grown. A great geography lesson and also a healthy eating activity—make it a rule that they can only have the stickers off fruit they eat!

GROW AN AVOCADO SEED

5+

*We all love eating avocados, but did you know how easy
it is to grow the seeds into a lovely potted plant?*

What You Need

- An avocado seed • Toothpicks
- Glass • Pot • Potting mix

What To Do

Next time you enjoy an avocado, keep the seed and wash it well. Carefully remove the dark brown covering over the seed. Push a few toothpicks around the middle of the seed and balance it in a glass full of water, with the water coming up to just below the toothpicks.

Place the glass on a windowsill and the children can check it each day. Make sure they add more water when necessary, so the bottom of the seed is always covered with water.

In time, the seed will split and roots will form, growing down into the water. Soon a sprout will grow from the top of the seed.

Now it is time for the children to help you plant the seed into a pot, using good quality potting mix.

Keep the plant pruned by picking out the top leaves and the avocado will grow into a lovely bushy plant to bring inside from time to time.

273

5+

LET'S FIND OUT

*Help your children develop their inquiring minds by posing
these questions about the insects they find in the garden.*

What You Need

- Insects from the garden • Glass jar with holes in the lid

What To Do

Take your children on an 'insect hunt' around the garden. Help them capture an insect such as an ant or a beetle in a glass jar with holes in the lid. Now pose some of these questions:

What does it eat? — Leaves, other insects, grains, nectar, wood or sap?

What does it look like? — Is it multi or one colour? Is it dull or shiny? Can it be camouflaged?

Where does it live? — In flowers, on leaves or stems, in plants or water?

How does it move? or in zig zags? — Does it fly, crawl, burrow? Does it fly quickly, slowly, straight

How many? — Wings? Legs? Feelers does it have?

Older children may like to start a 'bug book'. Photograph or help your children draw the insect, see if they can identify it and then list all the characteristics discovered. Have your children show their teacher at school. All this may lead on to an interesting project for the whole class.

LOOKING FOR RAINBOWS

5+

*Children love looking at rainbows. You can delight
them by showing them how to make their own!*

What You Need

- A prism (chandeliers have prisms) • Torch
- Bubble water and a bubble pipe or wand mirror
- Shallow plastic tray • White paper • Machine oil

What To Do

Look through a prism together to see a beautiful rainbow. Blow some bubbles in the sunlight and look for the rainbows. Take a bowl of water out into the sunlight, drop in a few drops of machine oil and, hey presto! Rainbows!

Another way to make a rainbow is to put a mirror in a bowl of water in the sunlight and look for the rainbows there. Or you can shine a torch on the mirror while your children hold a piece of paper to catch the rainbow.

Don't forget to tell them the old tale of the pot of gold at the end of the rainbow and talk about the colours that make up the rainbow—they may not know colours such as indigo or violet.

Then provide some new paints or felt pens so they can create their own colourful rainbow pictures.

ONION POWER

My children are always amused when Mummy cries when chopping up onions. They are not so amused when I put one near them! Ask your children to chop up an onion and explain what is happening to their eyes.

What You Need

- An onion • Chopping board • Knife

What To Do

When your children peel the onion and chop it, their eyes will begin to water. Why is it so?

Explain that onions contain a highly irritating oil that combines with the air when we are chopping them. This becomes a vapour that affects nerve glands that are actually in our noses, but connect to our eyes. This is how a strong smell or even a sneeze can make our eyes water.

Help your children to try some ways to see if you can stop onions making eyes water. Some people say to keep them in the refrigerator, or peel them under running water, or even peel them with sunglasses on! See what other creative solutions your children can come up with.

OVAL EGGS

Have your children ever wondered why eggs aren't round? This is one of the eternal questions children ask parents. Try this simple experiment together to discover why.

What You Need

- A hard-boiled egg • A tennis ball or other small round ball

What To Do

Put both the egg and the ball on the floor and roll them. Which is easier to roll? Can your children work out why?

Explain to them that if eggs were round they would roll so easily they could roll out of the nest. The oval shape is also stronger and less likely to break.

ROCKETS

Help your children understand about propulsion and what happens to air under pressure with this interesting experiment.

What You Need

- 2 chairs • Drinking straw • Masking tape
- Pieces of string about 2–2½ metres (6–7½ ft) long
- Balloon (as large and as long as you can find)

What To Do

Thread the string through the straw and tie the chairs together about two metres (six feet) apart. Move the chairs apart until the string is stretched tight. Next, blow up the balloon and hold it tight as you tape it to the straw. Then release the balloon! Your children will be fascinated by the result.

Explain that when you blew up the balloon, the air molecules were forced into it and, although we could not see them, they were tightly packed. When the balloon was released, the air escaped with so much force that the balloon was propelled along the string.

Explain that rockets use similar force, but not with air. Rockets use rocket fuel. Sky rockets that we see at fireworks displays use gunpowder as force, as do firearms.

SPIDERS

Help your child learn more about spiders and their importance in our environment.

What You Need

- A spider and its web to observe
- Spray paint • Paper

What To Do

Find a spider's web in the garden and watch it together for a few days. See what the spider does in the daytime. Then come out with a torch at night and observe its activity. Watch the small insects it has caught in the web and see how long the spider takes to eat them.

If you can find an old uninhabited web, you can make a web picture by lightly spraying the spider's web with white spray paint. Hold a piece of black paper behind the web and at the anchoring points of the web. The wet paint will stick the web onto the paper. Your children will be amazed by the spider's line work.

It's fun to go into the garden early in the morning also and watch any spider's web glistening with dew. Look at the shapes in the web and see how many squares, triangles, rectangles and even hexagons and pentagons the children can find.

Talk about safety and spiders also. Ensure that the children never try to touch a spider. See if you can find a book at the library about spiders and read it together.

STICK INSECTS

Stick insects fascinate children of all ages—and adults too! They come in a variety of colours and sizes, and are completely harmless.

What You Need

- A very large jar or shoebox with holes in the lid • Time

What To Do

Hunt through the garden or visit the local park and see if you and your children can find a stick insect. Some years there seem to be many more stick insects than others, so depending on when you do this activity you may find a stick insect quickly or hunt for ages!

Stick insects enjoy a variety of plants in the home garden, such as rose bushes and fruit trees. Show your children how to look carefully on the undersides of leaves and branches for a stick insect.

Some stick insects are quite small but others are enormous and can reach lengths of around 30 cm (12 in). As a rule, females are much larger than males.

Once your children find a stick insect, transfer it gently to the jar or shoe box, together with some fresh leaves from the plant you found it on. Sprinkle a few drops of water on the leaves.

Allow the children to keep this fascinating insect for a day or so and then return it to the place they found it.

Hint!

If you can't find a stick insect, you can buy a stick insect 'kit' containing eggs and food. Check stick insects out on the Internet, to find a place to purchase them.

TERRARIUM GARDEN

*A simple and inexpensive way to make a little garden
with your children—ideal for unit dwellers.*

What You Need

- Large plastic soft drink bottle with a black base • Craft knife
- Potting mix • Small plants or seeds

What To Do

Cut the soft drink bottle in half with a craft knife and then soak the bottom half in warm water until the clear plastic comes out of the black base. When this section is inverted and pushed into the black base, you have a simple but most effective terrarium to make a little garden in, with your children.

Fill the base with some good quality potting mix and plant together with small plants or seeds. Water it and then seal. Terrariums are best kept in a warm spot away from direct sunlight. They will only need watering every ten days as it is a sealed environment like a hot house, so be careful not to over-water.

Terrariums make ideal places to raise seeds in cooler climates, and to grow cuttings. Happy gardening!

WIND CHIMES

Help your children make these simple wind chimes, using objects from nature.
You will all take delight in their pretty, tinkly sounds on windy days.

What You Need

- Items found in nature such as bamboo, shells, seed pods, pieces of wood etc.
  - Small brass bells (can be purchased from craft shops and gift shops)
    - Fishing line or thin string • 1 or 2 sticks from the garden

---

What To Do

Help your children collect items from the garden, beach etc. to hang on the wind chimes. Then assemble them on pieces of fishing line or thin string. Thread the tiny brass bells on last. You will need to help with drilling holes or tying knots. Attach the strings to one or two sticks and tie a string handle on them, for hanging.

When the wind chimes are finished, hang them from a convenient tree branch and enjoy the music of the wind.

WORM HOUSE

It's easy to find a worm for your children to keep for a while, and watch.
Make a simple Worm House with your children so they can learn more
about these small animals.

What You Need

- Worms • Tall, thin jar
- Sand, earth, peat moss or compost

What To Do

Take your children and the tall, thin jar into the garden and fill the jar with layers of different coloured things like peat, sand, compost and, most importantly, earth containing lots of leaf mould. This is what the worms will eat. Make sure the bottle is kept cool and moist, but not wet.

Dig in the garden together until you find a worm. Put it on the top of the jar so your children have a good chance to observe it.

As the worm tunnels down through the layers it feeds on the earth. What it exudes is called the worm-cast. Your children will be able to watch the patterns the worm makes as it moves through the layers of dirt.

When your children have learnt all they can about worms, make sure you dig a hole together and place the worm back in the garden.

Find out more about worms from your local library or even invest in a worm farm to make great compost for the garden.

6+

BEANS

Beans are one of the quickest and easiest vegetables to grow.
They are great for first-time vegetable gardeners and your
children will love to eat the beans they grow!

What You Need

- Small pots • Potting mix
- Bean seeds (green beans are best for this activity)
- Pencils • Scrapbook

What To Do

Take your children to a nursery and let them choose the variety of beans they wish to grow. There are some good dwarf varieties available that grow quickly and crop heavily—they will give good results for children who are growing vegetables for the first time.

Help your children to plant one or two bean seeds into each small pot. They may like to have two or three pots each, so they get a good crop (remember that there have been health concerns associated with potting mix, so always keep the mix damp when working with it and everyone wash hands thoroughly afterwards).

Your children can water their beans every few days and they will delight in watching the young plants grow, flower and produce beans within a matter of weeks. If growing beans in cold weather it will be necessary to keep the pots inside, on a sunny windowsill. But if the plants are kept warm enough they will still flower and produce beans.

When the beans are ready to pick, help your children to cook them. They will readily eat vegetables they have grown themselves, even if they are usually fussy eaters!

BOTANICAL GARDENS

6+

*Most large towns and cities have wonderful Botanical Gardens
to visit with your children. Take a picnic lunch, some bread to feed the
ducks and birds (if it is allowed) and commune with nature.*

What You Need

- Time • Botanical Gardens

What To Do

Botanical Gardens are examples of excellence in gardening and, as a keen gardener, I love visiting them. But so do children and what a great way to help them appreciate trees, flowers and special types of gardens.

Many Botanical Gardens have very, very, old trees to gaze up at, wonderfully colourful annual displays and space to run and play. Most have water features and wild birds to feed and enjoy. They are places of beauty and tranquillity and, in our busy lives, these are often rare.

Do take your children to your nearest Botanical Garden regularly and they will grow up appreciating gardens of all types.

6+

MOON CHART

Teach your child about the phases of the moon by making a simple moon chart.

What You Need

- Paper • Pencils or felt pens • Time
- Clear night skies • Daily newspapers

What To Do

Check in the daily newspaper in the weather section, to work out when there will be a new moon. Most large daily newspapers have this information.

When you know there is going to be a new moon, take your children outside to see the tiny sliver and explain to them that at different times of the month we can see more or less of the moon from Earth. Help them divide their chart into around eight sections. Then they can draw the new moon in the first section and write the date beside it. You may need to help younger children with this.

Every few days, take your children outside and show them the moon. Discuss how it changes—first quarter, half-moon, full moon etc. Have your children draw what they see each time.

Your children will be fascinated by the waxing and waning moon. Who knows—it may start them off on a lifetime interest in astronomy!

MOONLIGHT HIKE

Take your family with you on a moonlight hike.

What You Need

- Torch • Clear moonlit night

What To Do

Put on your joggers and go for a moonlight walk in a nature reserve. You could all listen to the sounds of the night and try to identify noises you wouldn't hear in the daytime.

Stay very still and you might see some nocturnal animals, such as bats, owls, or even a fox.

Together, look at the shapes and colours of the night; observe how different the sky appears, look at flowers and trees, and look at the shapes of houses, cars and each other.

When you come home, read some books from the library about nocturnal creatures. Did you see any of them?

NIGHT SKIES

*Here is another simple astronomy activity you can
do to further your children's interest in space.*

What You Need

- Clear warm nights
- A simple star guide (from library)

What To Do

Go outside with your children at night and observe the sky together. Look at the stars and, using a star guide, see if you can find some star patterns.

See what other things you can observe at night; if you and your children are lucky, you may see shooting stars or tiny, bright satellites orbiting far above you.

Borrow some books from your local library and help your children learn more about our galaxy. You will be able to find out when the most likely times for meteor showers are from these books and your children will be thrilled if they see them.

Toy shops and newsagents sell luminous stars and moons. Make a 'night sky' on the ceiling of your children's room.

PARSLEY POTS

Parsley is a herb which supposedly cleans the blood and refreshes the palate. It also tastes great and makes a wonderful garnish. A pot of parsley really brightens up a kitchen windowsill.

What You Need

- Punnet of parsley plants • Potting mix
- Terracotta pots • Ribbon

What To Do

Parsley pots make terrific Christmas gifts for teachers or anyone else you know who enjoys cooking. Best of all, the children will enjoy helping make them and look after them.

Go to your local nursery or plant centre with the kids and buy the parsley punnets. There are usually about six plants per punnet, so work out how many you will need. Terracotta pots are inexpensive and come in all shapes and sizes, but a 15 cm (6 in) pot should be about the right size. If you don't have potting mix at home, buy some there also.

Because there are some health concerns about potting mix, help the children plant the seedlings and make sure it is moist and no dust escapes. One seedling per pot will suffice.

Water the seedlings daily, leave them in a sunny sheltered position and after a few days give them some liquid fertiliser, or long-acting fertiliser grains. In six weeks so they will make wonderful presents.

SHELL COLLECTIONS

Encourage your children to become collectors and begin life-long hobbies.
One of the simplest and cheapest things to collect is shells.

What You Need

- Shells

What To Do

Next time you go to the beach with the family take a bucket or a plastic container with a lid and go for a walk with the children to collect shells. Only collect shells that have no living things inside them.

When you return home the children can wash their shells and leave them to dry in the sun for a few days, to reduce odours.

It is worth buying or at least borrowing a good book on shells so the children can name and classify their shells.

Shell collections can be stored in boxes, glued with PVA glue onto strong cardboard or even framed for interesting wall decorations.

SHELL MOBILE

*Here is another fun mobile idea for your children to make. Keep holiday memories
alive by collecting shells and driftwood at the beach and make a shell mobile together.*

What You Need

- Pieces of driftwood • Shells with small holes in them • Fishing line

What To Do

Next time you are at the beach, collect as many shells as you can find that have small holes in
them. These are quite easy to find. Also see if you can find some interesting pieces of driftwood.

When you come home, help your children thread the shells with the fishing lines—you won't be
able to use a bodkin or tapestry needle as the holes in shells are usually too tiny.

Attach the threading to the driftwood and hang outside in the breeze. The delightful tinkling will
bring back lots of holiday memories.

SILK WORMS

Children are fascinated by the life cycle of these amazing little creatures.

What You Need

- Silk worms—try your local pet shop, look for ads in the paper, or ask at your local primary school. They are available around early spring
- A shoe box • Mulberry leaves

What To Do

If you are lucky enough to be given eggs, your children can watch the changes in the eggs. Mostly, however, you will be given the small silkworms. As they grow, the silkworms increase their weight hundreds of times. Older children will be able to measure and weigh (use a small set of kitchen scales) and graph the results.

Isolate one silkworm and keep a count of how many mulberry leaves it can eat in a day. Your children will also be able to observe the caterpillars moulting—when the silkworms become very inactive as their skin is stretched and while they are getting ready to shed it. Look at the changes in the new skin—it will be darker and wrinkly to allow room for more growth.

The next most fascinating stage is when the silkworms begin to spin their cocoons. The cocoons must not be bumped or handled, but just watched for the next three weeks. Finally, the adult moth will emerge but, in doing so, it destroys the cocoon. Use some of the cocoons for spinning, but keep the rest so you will have a supply of eggs for next year's silk worms.

Put all the moths in a clean, dry shoe box in a cool place. Now the moths will mate and lay eggs. The male moth then dies. The female moth also dies, after laying approximately 500 eggs. Keep the eggs in a cool cupboard until next year, when the cycle will begin again.

SILK WORMS—SPINNING THE COCOON

As well as watching the life cycle of the silk worm, your children will enjoy spinning the silk from some of the cocoons. Make a simple spinner with directions below.

What You Need

- Lead pencil • Old cotton reel
- Drinking glass • Wood glue

What To Do

When I was a child my father made me a silk spinner from four pieces of dowel, but this simpler version works just as well.

Push the pencil through the hole in the cotton reel and glue in place.

Put the cocoon into a glass that is half filled with warm water. You'll then be able to easily peel off the loose outside layer of the cocoon. Next, find the end of the thread and wind it around the cotton reel. Put the cocoon back in the glass and begin winding.

Keep some of the silk on each cocoon to protect the pupa, but it's also a good idea to keep a few cocoons unwound to be sure to hatch out some moths.

Take the silk off carefully and tie together to form a narrow piece about 30 cm (12 in) long. It makes a great book mark.

Show your children some real silk—perhaps look in a haberdashery for some silk fabrics.

Go to the library together to find some books about the silk industry in China. You'll all learn something new!

SKIN DEEP

As we age, our skin loses it elasticity and becomes older and lined. With a magnifying glass your children will enjoy seeing the differences in skin as it ages.

What You Need

• A magnifying glass • Children and adults of different ages

What To Do

Take a magnifying glass along to a family gathering and your children will be astonished by the differences between older and younger hands.

Explain to them that skin is actually an organ of the body and expands and contracts as you grow and lose weight. Unfortunately, as we age, our skin becomes less elastic and will not so easily contract to its original shape. Let them examine their own hands, then yours, then Grandma's and Grandpa's. Apply some hand lotion to your hands and let them see if this makes any difference.

Don't forget to remind them that the sun can damage skin and, to keep it looking young longer, they must always remember to use sunscreen.

SNAILS

Help your children learn more about these fascinating creatures.

What You Need
- Snails from the garden
- Aquarium or very large glass jar

What To Do

When snails invade your garden, before you reach for the snail bait, collect a few for your children to observe and study for a few days. It's fun to go on a snail hunt together at night with a torch—you'll find lots more that way.

Put the snails you have collected in the aquarium and give them some food—lettuce is ideal—in fact that is what they are given to cleanse them before being eaten.

Your children will enjoy seeing the snail's large foot as it travels across the glass using its wave-like contractions. Observe the mucous trail that is left, which protects the snail from sharp surfaces. Did you know snails can crawl over very sharp objects without being hurt? Put a razor blade or sharp knife in the aquarium and watch.

Snail races are fun too! Mark the snails with different coloured stickers on their shells and put them on a marked path. Time the snail to see how far they can move in a minute.

Your children will be fascinated to learn that snails are considered to be gourmet fare in France and Japan. If they are adventurous eaters, buy a jar of snails from a good deli and cook them gently in butter and garlic. Yummy!

Make your children's snails the focus of a school project or talk to the class. Go to the local library together and find out more interesting facts about snails. Their classmates and teachers will be fascinated too!

SOLAR SYSTEM MOBILE

When your children really become fascinated by outer space and our solar system, help them make a solar system mobile to hang above their bed.

What You Need

- An old umbrella • Yellow paint • Fishing line • Cardboard
- Silver spray paint or aluminium foil
- Polystyrene balls (available in different sizes from craft shops)

What To Do

Together, remove all the fabric from an old umbrella. Then make the 'solar system'. Paint the largest polystyrene ball yellow and cover the others with silver aluminium foil, or spray paint them silver. Cut out some cardboard stars and moons.

Borrow some books about space from your local library to get the exact positioning of all the planets, then attach them all with fishing line to the umbrella.

Buy a pack of 'glow in the dark' stars from a toyshop and stick these to the ceiling, too. Your children will want to spend a lot of time lying on their bed!

SPRING BULBS

Here is a great long-term activity that will help teach your children about the life cycle of plants over the seasons.

What You Need

• Large plant pots • Potting mix • Bulbs of your children's choice (a large variety available from nurseries but daffodils are always popular) • Pencils • Scrapbook • Time

What To Do

Explain to your children that some plants change dramatically with the seasons and that bulbs, in particular, have a life-cycle that depends on the weather and time of the year. Take your children to a nursery in autumn and help them choose some pretty spring bulbs—they will love looking at the different pictures on the bulb packets.

Tell your children that the bulb is now dormant, or 'sleeping', but that inside the bulb is a beautiful flower just waiting to come out in the warmer weather! Help them to plant their bulbs in large plant pots (remember that potting mix has been associated with some health problems, so make sure it's damp when you use it and everyone wash their hands thoroughly afterwards).

Your children can now keep their potted bulbs in a safe place over winter. Have them keep a scrapbook, recording the progress of their bulbs. They can write the date they planted them and draw a picture to match. Then, in late winter, the bulbs will begin to shoot. Your children will take great delight in recording their bulbs' progress in their scrapbooks, and will be amazed at the life-cycle of their plants.

SUNSHINE FACTS

We all know how important the sun is for life on Earth. Help your children discover this for themselves with this simple experiment.

What You Need

- Birdseed • Small pots
- Potting mix • Shoe box

What To Do

Help your children fill the pots with some potting mix and sow the soil liberally with the birdseed (don't forget to keep potting mix damp when using it and everyone wash their hands thoroughly after using it). Place outside in a sunny spot in the garden or on a balcony and water regularly. When the little plants are strong and green it is time to begin the experiment.

Put a couple of the pots into a dark cupboard—remember to keep watering them regularly, though.

Place another pot into a shoe box with the lid on and make a small hole in one end so this is the only light source for that plant. Again, remember to water regularly so the plant doesn't die.

Return the other pots to the sunny spot in the garden again.

In a week or so, check all the pots to see what has happened. The plants in the dark cupboard will have grown tall and spindly and probably turned yellow without sunlight. The plants in the box will have grown towards the light but the ones in the sunny garden should be lush and healthy.

This shows the children that an adequate supply of sunlight is necessary for healthy plant growth.

USING THE STREET DIRECTORY

Use your local street directory to help your children learn about maps.

What You Need

- Street directory or map of your local area

What To Do

Before you go for walks with your children, or short drives in the car together, look up where you are going in your street directory. Work out a route together and take it with you. Check it as you turn corners and change directions. Look for local landmarks such as schools, churches, shopping centres and parks on the map.

As your children gain mapping skills, make them the 'navigator' for longer trips to places you have not been before. Keep your cool! You will probably get lost a few times, but many adults go through their whole lives without ever developing a good sense of direction. Help your children gain mastery over this important life skill in a fun and relaxing way.

6

WATTLE SEED OLYMPICS

*This game will help your children gain an
understanding of how plants survive and reproduce.*

What You Need

- Wattle seed pods

What To Do

After your wattle trees have flowered in winter they produce seed pods. Most of these seed pods are aerodynamically designed to spread in the wind over a very wide area.

Collect lots of seed pods with your children and take them up on a verandah (always watch young children carefully in high places).

Let the seed pods go and watch carefully to see which go the furthest, which take the longest and shortest time to hit the ground, which twist the most and perhaps, which hit a certain target you have marked earlier.

If you are doing this on a windy day, the seed pods will get blown further and your children will have the opportunity to see how wind helps spread seeds.

When you go for walks, or to parks with your children, take a bag to collect other interesting 'flying' seeds.

COCKROACHES

*While most adults find cockroaches fairly repulsive and suggest
dirty surroundings, children are usually quite interested in them!*

What You Need

- A torch

What To Do

We know that cockroaches can and do live in most of our homes, especially those of us who live in warmer parts. Help your children discover that they also live out of doors by going on a cockroach hunt at night.

Take a torch as, like most insects, they are attracted to artificial light. You can often find them under piles of rotting leaves, mulch or wood chips in your garden. The children will need to look carefully as the cockroaches will be well camouflaged. See if they can spot female cockroaches with their strange looking egg sacks attached to their bodies.

Summer time is the best time for trying to spot cockroaches and some do fly at night, especially in warmer and tropical places. Encourage your children to observe how they move and how their long antennae seem to be constantly shaking and quivering.

See if you can find out any more interesting facts about cockroaches from books in your home, or borrow some from your local library.

Did you know that many lizards eat cockroaches and that palaeontologists have found cockroach fossils that date back further than the time of the dinosaurs—back as far as 300 million years!

I guess we can assume that we have them with us forever!

CRYSTAL MAKING

Help your children understand more about how rocks are formed by making some easy crystals from sugar.

What You Need

- 2 cups sugar • Food colouring • 1 cup boiling water
- Shallow bowl • Wooden kebab sticks or pieces of string

What To Do

Carefully stir the sugar into the boiling water, add a few drops of food colouring and let it cool to room temperature.

Your children will enjoy arranging the kebab sticks or pieces of string in the bowl. Then they slowly and carefully pour on the sugar solution. Cover and let it stand for a few days. More and more crystals will form as the mixture stands.

Hint!

Instead of adding the food colouring at the start, your children could add drops of different food colouring with an eye dropper to the crystals to make a garden-like effect.

CYCLONES

Show your children how a cyclone forms by making one in a bottle.

What You Need

- Two empty clear plastic 2 litre soft drink bottles • Connecting piece (available from geographic shops, science centres, some toy stores)
- Insulating tape • Food colouring

What To Do

Wash the bottles out and discard the tops. Fill one bottle about two-thirds full of water. Add a few drops of food colouring at this stage, as this makes it easier for the children to see the water swirling. Screw the connection piece onto the bottle containing the water and then upend the other bottle and screw it onto the top. Tape securely with the insulating tape to make sure the water doesn't leak.

Help your children make the cyclone by swirling the water hard in the bottom bottle and then turning it upside down so the water is now in the top. Watch the water form a cyclone as it drains to the lower bottle.

See what happens if you swirl the water in the opposite direction next time.

7+

CYCLONE WATCH

Expand your children's interest in cyclones and weather patterns by carrying out a cyclone watch together.

What You Need

- Paper • An atlas • Tracing paper
- Coloured pens or pencils

What To Do

Using tracing paper, help the kids trace their own large map of the world onto a large piece of paper or cardboard.

Watch the weather reports together each night on television or read them in your daily paper to see where cyclones are developing.

As each cyclone forms, help your children to draw it on their map and name it. Use a different colour for each cyclone and help them gradually plot its path. Make bigger cyclones larger on the map than smaller ones.

By the end of summer the children will have a fascinating map and a great deal more knowledge about weather maps and weather conditions.

Who knows, one of them may be a meteorologist one day!

FLOWER CHAINS

Make some beautiful flower chains with the children.

What You Need

- Flowers • Fishing line for threading

What To Do

When we were children we loved making simple clover chains by picking clover with long stems and then simply tying them together. Show your children how to do this.

Another easy flower chain to make is a frangipani lei, made by threading frangipani flowers onto fishing line. Remember though, that frangipanis are very poisonous and the children must wash their hands well when they have finished threading.

Other flowers can be used for threading but you may have to use needles threaded with the fishing line or strong thread. Show the children how to push the needles through the flowers. Daisies look lovely threaded as a chain.

Perhaps they would like to make a flower chain to give to a friend, or to wear on a special occasion.

7+

GROW YOUR OWN GRAPE VINE

Grape vines are beautifully ornamental as well as a practical addition to any garden. The children will enjoy watching their vine as it changes with the seasons.

What You Need

- A grape vine plant or cutting

What To Do

Visit your local nursery to ask for some advice about the best variety of grape for your area.

Grapes are heavy and vigorous climbers and will need a strong structural support. They are ideal for growing over pergolas or courtyard covers as they will provide wonderful green summer shade but, when pruned back hard, will let in the winter sun.

The children will love watching the seasons change and the new bunches of grapes grow and then colour. If you buy a suitable variety you could even have a go at juicing them and making some delicious grape juice.

Find a recipe for delicious Greek dolmades and stuff some grape leaves with the children for a yummy meal.

A grape vine is a great addition to any garden.

MINIATURE GARDENS

My sister and I loved making miniature gardens when we were children. It is an excellent way to begin gardening. Introduce your kids to these and they too, may be as enchanted by them as we were.

What You Need

- Containers for the gardens—large plant pot saucers work really well
- Potting mix • Tiny plants • Small toys or figurines
- Pebbles or small stones • Mirrors

What To Do

Help your children fill their saucers with potting mix (remember to keep potting mix damp and everyone wash their hands thoroughly after using it, as there have been health concerns associated with potting mix).

Next, the children will enjoy planting small plants from the garden in their miniature gardens—mosses are terrific for the 'grass'. Then they add the interesting bits—the pebbles, mirrors for ponds and some of their small toys to create a fascinating small world.

They will enjoy watering and looking after their own tiny gardens and, like all gardeners, will enjoy changing aspects of their own little 'patches'.

Perhaps they could take their miniature garden to school as a special project, or for a class talk.

NATURE COLLAGE

Next time you take the children for a bush walk or a picnic they might enjoy collecting some materials for a nature collage (remember not to take anything home from a national park though).

What You Need

• Natural items such as mosses, leaves, twigs, bark, flowers, grasses and seeds • A piece of strong cardboard, polystyrene tray, or a piece of wood • PVA glue or a glue gun

What To Do

Art framers will often let you have off-cuts of cardboard that they use for framing and these are perfect for making nature collages. Otherwise a washed meat tray or a piece of thin wood is fine also.

Your children will enjoy making the picture—encourage them to make it look as close to nature as possible. If they are using glue they can apply it with a small brush or cotton bud, but if they are using a glue gun, it needs close adult supervision.

When the collage is finished let it dry in a safe place for a few days. It can be hung or displayed standing in a plate stand and makes a lovely reminder of a family day out.

POTATO FEAST

7+

Nothing tastes as good as freshly dug baby potatoes from your own garden and they are so easy to grow. Show the children how to do this and they can grow some and sell them to Mum for pocket money!

What You Need

• Seed potatoes • Potting mix • Compost

What To Do

Although potatoes do sprout and we have often found potatoes growing in the garden from old ones thrown out, it is better to start with special seed potatoes. You can buy these from your local nursery or garden centre.

Potatoes can be planted twice a year—usually in late winter and late summer. Help the children thoroughly dig over a section of garden and add lots of lovely compost from your compost bin or heap. If you live in a flat or unit, they can grow their potatoes in a large pot or even a black plastic rubbish bag (with a few holes pokes in the bottom for drainage). Just make sure you use a good quality potting mix with lots of mulch included in the mix (remembering to keep potting mix damp while using it and wash hands thoroughly after use, due to health concerns associated with it).

To help your potatoes have the best possible start, leave them in a tray or shoe box lid in a sunny spot on the balcony or a window sill until they begin to sprout. Then plant out the potatoes about a metre apart in the garden or two or three in a large pot or rubbish bag. Water them regularly. Potatoes prefer heavy watering at regular intervals but need good drainage. They should also be fertilised periodically.

In three to four months the potato plants will begin to die off and this is the time to dig them up and discover the wonderful potato treasure under the ground.

Yum! Potatoes in their jackets for dinner!

RAINDROP SPOTS

Help your children learn more about rain with this simple experiment.

What You Need

- Blotting paper (available from newsagents)
- Pens • Rain

What To Do

The next time it begins to rain, take some sheets of blotting paper out into the garden and hold them out in the rain. Bring them in and help the children draw around the outlines of the rain drops.

Ask them questions like:

Are the rain drops all the same shape and size?
Do they change when the rain is heavier or lighter?
How long does it take for a whole sheet of blotting paper to be soaked?
Does light rain sound different from heavy rain falling on a sheet of blotting paper?

Collect some rain in a see-through container and observe how clear the water is.

Add some soap to it and compare it to tap water. Which one lathers the most? Which one is the softest?

Children will be really interested in these simple experiments.

SAVING SEEDS

Recycling can be fun! Help the children recycle seeds and save money.

What You Need

• Fruit and vegetables • Colander • Baking tray

What To Do

Encourage the children to save seeds that they can use to plant for their vegetable gardens. They will enjoy watching them grow into new plants.

When you eat fruit and vegetables that you could grow in your own garden, show the children how to save the seeds. They could save tomato, rockmelon, watermelon, pumpkin, peas, beans, and many other seeds.

They need to wash the seeds carefully and take off any fruit or vegetable matter so that the seeds won't rot. Then put them into a strainer or colander (depending on the size of the seeds) and run lots of cool water through them.

Dry the seeds on a tray on a sunny windowsill, or on a table in the sun. When they are completely dry store them in well sealed screw top jars or plastic containers.

Label the containers with the name of the seeds and the date.

The children will enjoy growing their own fruit and vegetables from their seeds.

SUNFLOWER MEASURING

Grow some tall sunflowers with the children and have
a competition to see whose flower grows the tallest.

What You Need

- Sunflower seeds
- Garden stakes

What To Do

Sunflowers need a sunny spot in the garden. If you don't have somewhere suitable to grow them they will grow well in large pots. Sunflowers grow very fast and in just 6 months will easily grow up to 3 m (9 ft).

Dig over a patch of the garden for the sunflowers or alternatively, fill the pots with good quality potting mix. Add compost to the garden or pots. Plant the sunflower seeds according to the directions on the packet so they have room to grow and spread.

When the plants reach $^1/_2$ m ($1^1/_2$ ft) they will need staking with a garden stake or bamboo cane.

Measure the sunflowers each week and do some simple graphing with the children to record their growth. See whose plant is the tallest when the first flower appears.

Sunflower seeds can be saved and planted again next year!

TAKE IT APART

Develop your children's interest in how things
work by letting them take things apart.

What You Need

• Screwdriver • A pair of pliers • Old appliances

What To Do

If your kids are interested in how things work (and there are very few who aren't), develop their inquiring minds by letting them take apart simple broken appliances instead of throwing them out.

Always keep safety a high priority. Cut off any power cords first and, of course, appliances that must remain sealed such as TV's, refrigerators, microwaves and freezers are not to be touched.

However, items such as bike parts, broken toys, clocks, watches, phones, old radios (not with tubes), small appliances such as toasters and hairdryers, torches and old record players can all be taken apart and examined. Make sure there is always an adult around to supervise and to help if necessary.

Components also make great art. Maybe when they've finished checking out why the clock no longer works, they might like to make a robot or a super machine artwork out of all the bits.

7+

THE ANATOMY OF A FLOWER

Older children will be interested in the different parts of a flower.

What You Need

- Different sorts of flowers to observe • A magnifying glass

What To Do

Children need to learn that although flowers look beautiful, they are also an essential stage in a plant's growth. When pollen from one flower reaches another of the same species the plant can produce seeds. Explain to your children that although pollen can be spread by wind or water, it is most often spread by animals and insects. Insects, small mammals and birds all help in spreading the pollen of flowering plants. Show them some bees gathering pollen and nectar.

Your children will enjoy looking at different flowers under a magnifying glass (or microscope if you have one) and identifying the parts.

Petal—attracts insects
Sepal—the green petals that protect the bud at the base of the flower
Pistil—the female part of the flower. The pistil has three parts: the sticky top stigma traps pollen from other plants; the stalk or the style holds the stigma'; the ovary contains the plant's eggs which develop into seeds when fertilised.

Stamen—the male part of the flower. The stamen has two parts; the anther produces pollen; the filament holds up the anther.

Your children will be fascinated by plants. Encourage their interest and you may one day have a botanist in the family.

TYRE MOUNDS

7

Old tyres are readily available from tyre depots and garages and make great instant gardens and mounds.

What You Need

- Old tyres • Sand or soil
- Manure • Straw • Plants

What To Do

The children will enjoy rolling the tyres to make a mound in the garden or position them against a slope to help retain it. Put down some tyres, fill them with mixture of sand or soil, manure and straw and then position more tyres on the top and fill them and so on.

Finally you will have a mound with sections of tyre visible to use for the plantings—little mini-gardens.

Herbs are ideal to use for planting the sunny side of the tyre mound. Some herbs such as mints can tend to dominate a herb garden, but by planting a different variety of herb in each tyre they will each have their own space.

On the shady side of the mound you can plant annuals with the children or plants that need a little shade.

This is a big gardening project but one that you will all enjoy doing together and admiring and eating the finished results.

7+ WORLD ENVIRONMENT DAY

It is essential our children are aware of the importance of caring for the environment.

What You Need

- Time

What To Do

World Environment Day falls on 6th June and it is a good opportunity to help your children realise that they, too, can contribute to a healthy environment. Do some brainstorming together about ways you as a family could use less power, recycle more and generally be more aware of looking after the environment.

Many environmental organisations have special events and open days on World Environment Day. Take the children along to these and help increase their understanding and commitment for environmental issues.

They cannot be too young to understand that we all have a role to play in making sure our world stays as clean and natural as possible for future generations.

BIRDS IN YOUR GARDEN

8+

*Encourage your children to have an interest in birds
by 'birdscaping' your garden with their help.*

What You Need

- Information from local libraries, council, nurseries
  about native plants that grow best in your area
  - A selection of native plants

What To Do

The best way to encourage birds into your garden is to grow plants that attract birds. Unfortunately, many natural habitats of native birds are being destroyed by new housing developments and industrial sites.

To attract birds to your garden you need to provide food, water, nesting places and shelter. Birds can be attracted back to an area by the careful selection of trees and shrubs that will provide a selection of food throughout the year. Enlist your neighbours' help in your project and, over a period of time, you will see many more birds in your local area.

Join the Parents Club at your children's school and also encourage them to grow bird-attracting plants. Your local council may assist with this by providing plants free of charge.

Gardens do not happen overnight, but your children will love to help you 'birdscape' your garden by planting trees and shrubs that will encourage a wide variety of birds to visit your garden.

BUILD A POND

One of the schools I visit made a wonderful pond in their grounds last year, with the help of the children. They had raised frogs from tadpoles and, when the tadpoles were nearly ready to turn into frogs, they were released into their pond. Every time I visited, the children proudly took me to see their pond.

What You Need

- The garden hose • Spade • Pond liner (available from nurseries, hardware stores and garden shops)
- Sand • Rocks for edging • Water plants

What To Do

Garden ponds are best made out in the open as they will become polluted with too many falling leaves. Choose a spot in the garden with the children and mark out the diameter with the garden hose. Cut the turf carefully with a spade to use elsewhere and then the children can help dig out the hole for the pond. Make the bottom in a few levels; line it with the sand and smooth out carefully. Next, cover with the liner and carefully mould it to fit the shape of the pond. Be very careful not to make any holes in the liner as you work.

Cover the edges of the liner with soil and then add rocks around the edge of the pool to make it look as natural as possible. Place the water plants in pots and position them just below the surface of the water.

Finally, fill the pond with water and allow it to stand for a few weeks before adding any fish or other pond creatures. It is a good idea to place a garden seat beside the pond so you can sit and enjoy it with the children.

BUSHWALKING

Take the family bushwalking and enjoy the beauty of the great outdoors.

What You Need

- Backpacks • Water bottles • Sensible shoes, clothing and hats • Insect spray and sunscreen
- A set of binoculars for watching birds and animals

What To Do

Bushwalking is something you can do with all the family. However, as your children grow older you will be able to plan longer hikes. It's a great way to keep everyone in the family fit and to appreciate nature. If you are not sure about good bushwalking areas where you live, contact your local National Parks office. They can give you lots of useful information about bushwalking and also let you know about the birds, animals and plants you may be likely to see on each walk.

Encourage all the family to take turns carrying backpacks with food, drinks and water, so the load is shared. If the National Parks office can supply you with maps, it's great to take one along together with a compass, and let the children gain some practical experience in map reading. A small guide to birds is also something I like to take along on long bushwalks, as I enjoy trying to identify birds spotted on the hike.

It's great to look at the natural world with the children and see how wonderful nature is as a landscaper. Creeks and ponds are another source of interest. Our son still talks about the big eel we spotted in a creek on a bushwalk last year.

Take the children to enjoy the serenity and beauty. Refresh their souls and spirit and enjoy fresh air and family time together. Best of all it's free!

CARNIVOROUS PLANTS

Your children will be fascinated by the amazing world of carnivorous plants!

What You Need

- Carnivorous plants (available from most good nurseries)

What To Do

The image of animal eating plants has inspired science fiction books and movies for decades. They are not all fantasies—there really are plants that actually catch and eat insects. Many carnivorous plants come from swampy areas which are low in nutrients, so many essential elements come from trapping and breaking down the insects.

One of the best known carnivorous plants is the venus fly trap (Dionaea muscipula) which has a hinged leaf and attracts flies. When the flies are inside they move fine hairs which then trigger the trap to close and trap the fly. Other well known carnivorous plants are the pitcher plants which attract insects with sweet nectars. Eventually, the insects fall into the pitcher and find it impossible to crawl back out.

Carnivorous plants are easy to grow and look after at home, and the kids will be fascinated. Many nurseries stock the plants and you will need to plant them in a container at home and try to replicate the boggy conditions they grow in naturally. Ask your nursery for the best potting mix or add lots of peat moss to retain the water naturally.

The children will soon become experts on carnivorous plants.

DESERT GARDENS

Most botanical gardens have sections where you
can take the children to view arid gardens.

What You Need

- Large shallow clay pot with a saucer • Small stones or gravel
- Cacti potting mix or regular potting mix with sand or grit added
- Rocks • Cacti and succulent plants • Thick gardening gloves

What To Do

Cacti gardens need little water and look best in a wide but shallow planter.

Help the children fill the container with the special potting mix or add some sand and shell grit to regular potting mix so it is not too heavy. Remind the children that these plants survive in very dry conditions and need well drained soil.

They will enjoy adding some stones to the pot for decoration and then add their selection of small cacti and other succulent plants. Nurseries will have a selection to choose from, or perhaps you have friends or family with cacti or succulent gardens who will be happy to let the children have some small cuttings or plants.

When the plants are arranged to their liking, they can sprinkle on the small stones or gravel for ground cover. During the summer the cacti garden will still need regular watering—but don't over-water. Show the children how to feel the soil with the tip of a finger to see if it is moist enough. In winter, however, remind them to water sparingly, probably only about once a month or the plant will rot away.

They will really enjoy growing their own desert gardens.

321

DRAW A TREE

*Older children who enjoy drawing will like drawing
a tree throughout the four seasons of the year.*

What You Need

- A tree that changes with the seasons
- Pencils • Paper

What To Do

This activity may be more difficult if you live in the tropics or warmer parts. However, in cooler climates where trees change with the seasons, encourage your child to draw the same tree at different times of the year, in summer, autumn, winter and spring. If the tree flowers, it will be especially interesting.

Children should be encouraged to draw from life as this creates an awareness of their environment.

GARDENING DIARY

8+

*Encourage an interest in gardening and the environment
by helping your children make a gardening diary.*

What You Need

- A good quality scrapbook or drawing book
- Glue, pencils, other drawing materials

What To Do

Encourage your children to take an interest in the garden by making a gardening diary together.

Use a double page for each month of the year and they can draw, paint or press flowers that bloom in the garden at that time to put in the section for that month.

Use gardening books you have at home, or access your local library for information about the plants they have featured. They may like to include where the plants originate, any special horticultural needs they have and their ideal growing conditions.

Encourage your children to look in other gardens or parks for plants they like that bloom in particular months, which could be added to your garden also.

The plant diary could be used as a school project or a special topic for a talk at school. This could begin a life-long love of plants and gardens in your children. Who knows—perhaps one of them may be a botanist one day!

8+

GENE POWER

*Genetics are big news in today's world, with new genetic breakthroughs
being discovered almost daily. Help your children understand what
genes are and how they affect us all.*

What You Need

• Pencil • Paper

What To Do

Help your children list all the members of your immediate family on the top of a large piece of paper. Under each family member help them think of physical characteristics of that person—their eye colour, hair colour, hair type (curly, wavy or straight), ear shape (detached or undetached lobes), and perhaps even whether they can curl their tongue.

Remind your children that all of these characteristics are inherited and that we have dominant and recessive genes. Work out how individual family members are similar and yet different.

Remind your children that genetics is the science of why living things behave and look the way they do. Inside each cell are tiny chromosomes which carry different genetic messages and help make us what we are. Explain to your children that they receive a mixture of genes from both parents and they can see sometimes which parent provided which characteristic. 'Thanks, Dad, for the big nose!'

GROWING BABY FERNS

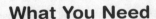

8+

*Show your children how to collect the spores from ferns
and grow some baby ferns to plant out in the garden.*

What You Need

- Thick white paper • Potting mix rich in humus • Pots

What To Do

Ferns grow in every size from minute ground-hugging plants to giant tree ferns and climbers. They mostly love shady places and prefer a cool moist atmosphere under trees. Grow them in well-drained soil rich in humus. They can be propagated by dividing clumps, but it is much more fun to collect the spores and the children grow new baby ferns.

Look at your ferns to see if there are any small brownish clusters of spores on the underside of some of the fronds. Pick the fronds and, with the children, lay them on the sheets of white paper for a day or so in a protected place until some of the spores have dropped onto the paper.

Fill several small pots or plastic containers with potting mix rich in humus and sprinkle the spore paper over them. The children will need to keep them moist but not wet, in a cool, shady part of the garden.

Watch carefully to see the new baby ferns beginning to grow. In time the children will be able to plant out the new ferns into the garden and they will feel a wonderful sense of accomplishment when they rear their own baby ferns!

If you have rainforests close to your home, encourage the children's interest in ferns by doing some bushwalking and seeing all the different specimens of ferns on the forest floor, in the rainforest canopy and clinging to the trees. Some rainforests have whole clusters of wonderful tree ferns.

8+

INSECT TRAPS

The children build an insect trap in the garden.

What You Need

- Small plastic container • Small garden trowel • Stones
- Piece of wood, bark or flat large stone

What To Do

Help your children select a spot in the garden that is unlikely to be disturbed by other family activities.

Dig a hole that is deep enough and big enough for the plastic container to sit in. Put the container in the hole and replace enough soil so the top of the container is level with the ground. Place some stones around the edge and then balance a larger flat stone or a piece of wood or bark on the top.

Leave the trap overnight and check with the children to see if any insects have been caught. If the trap hasn't worked perhaps you could put a small piece of bread soaked in honey in there and see if this attracts any visitors.

The children will enjoy looking at any small creatures with a magnifying glass to see all their features.

Don't forget to let any insects go after the children have finished studying them. All insects have a role to play in the mini-ecosystem of our gardens.

NATURE DIARIES

8+

Encourage your children's interest in and knowledge of the environment by helping them keep a Nature Diary.

What You Need
- Notebook • Pencil
- Coloured felt pens or pencils

What To Do

Every time you visit a park or botanical garden with your children, encourage them to take along their Nature Diaries.

Help them make a list of the different types of animals and plants that they see there. Later, you may be able to help them discover to which species those flora and fauna belonged by referring to books at home or in the library. It is important to use correct terminology with children.

Encourage them to note down which animals and plants were associated together and what the animals were eating.

If you visit the same places at different times of the year, encourage them to consult their Nature Diaries and note down any changes they observe.

Sometimes the children will see something very special and unusual, such as a tree covered with fungi. Take along your camera and photograph anything really special for them to add to their diaries. Encourage them to develop their drawing skills by drawing animals or birds they see. If you can't identify the animal or bird look it up in reference books later.

Activities like this will encourage a love of the environment in your children.

8

ORIENTEERING

Orienteering is a very popular sport world wide and is great for teaching children how to use a compass, as well as for fitness.

What You Need

- Compass • Maps • Paper
- Pen • Space to run a course

What To Do

Work out a track that you could take the children on to try some simple orienteering. National parks and state forests are ideal, as are local bush areas. Buy a map of the area to study with the children.

Set out the day before and work out a route; leave some markers under logs, stones, on bushes and so on. Of course, you must disturb the natural environment as little as possible. Mark the compass reading of each station for the children to follow.

The children begin with the first clue giving them the compass readings. With your help, they look it up on the map and set out. When they read the next clue, they look it up and so forth.

If all this sounds too complicated, it could be an idea to enquire if there is an Orienteering Club in your area and take the children along to participate. A fun, healthy family activity to try together.

SOLAR POWER

8+

Kids today are very environmentally conscious and are truly concerned about saving fossil fuel, and conserving our natural resources. Try this simple experiment to find out which materials absorb heat best and see if you can make some changes with your kids to the way your household uses heating fuels.

What You Need

- Pencil and paper • A variety of objects such as a dark house-brick, white vinyl, curtain lining, carpet square, a ceramic tile, aluminium foil and white paper

What To Do

This activity is best done on a hot, sunny day. Put all the objects chosen for the experiment out in the full sun. Come back in a couple of hours and see which objects are the hottest and which are the coolest. The children can order the heat-absorbing properties of each material from the most effective to the least effective.

Talk about ideas they have to make your home cooler in summer and warmer in winter. Go for a walk together and see how many houses in your area have solar heaters on their roof. You may even see some homes with solar heating for swimming pools on their roofs.

Think of ways your family can save power—always wash clothes on sunny days so you don't use the clothes dryer, or have a lap rug each in winter instead of using the heater; or turn off your electric blanket when you get into bed instead of leaving it on all night! Your children will be able to think of many others.

WEATHER INFORMATION

Encourage your older children's interest in the environment by helping them set up a weather station and recording and measuring each day's weather.

What You Need

- Strong cardboard • 2 broom handles
- Thermometer • Large tin • Ruler

What To Do

The weather station will need a rain gauge, a wind vane and a thermometer.

Attach the tin with suitable glue to the side or top of a broom handle and bury in the ground in an open part of the garden. Make sure it is firm enough not to be knocked over by strong winds. Your children will need a ruler to place in the tin to measure rainfall—a simple rain gauge.

To make the wind vane, you need a piece of strong cardboard about 15 cm (6 in) square. Mark each corner with the initials for the compass directions of North, South, East and West. Make a hole in the centre of the card so a broom handle fits in snugly and cut an arrow out of strong cardboard to attach to the top of the wind vane. Attach it so it will swing freely and point to the positions on the card. Bury it in the garden and use the early morning sun or a compass to make sure you have the correct positions.

Your children are then ready to begin measuring things like the amount of rainfall each month, the daily temperature, cloud formations, wind directions, and the amount of daylight hours. Help them graph their findings. Their teacher will also be most interested in this project!

SPORTS
SKILLS

BALL CHASES

A fun throwing game to play with a group of children.

What You Need

- A group of children • Two or more soft balls

What To Do

The children join hands to form a circle and then drop their hands. Space the children 1 m (3 ft) apart. Explain to them that they are going to be passing two balls around the circle and they have to see if the second ball can overtake the one in front.

Begin one ball and then, when it has been passed by a few children, begin the second ball.

The children really concentrate and this helps develop their throwing and catching skills.

BALL SWEEP

A fun game to play at a party, with a group of children, or with the family.

What You Need

- Brooms • Large rubber balls • Cardboard boxes

What To Do

Each player has a ball, a broom and a box to sweep his ball into. Spread the players out on the drive or in the backyard and when you say 'go' the players have to sweep their balls down to their boxes, which have been placed some distance away, as fast as they can.

The first player to sweep the ball into their box is the winner.

A variation on this game, if you don't have enough balls or brooms for all the players, is to divide the children into relay teams. The first player in each team sweeps the ball into the box. The next player sweeps it out and back to the start and so on. Relays are lots of fun to play with children.

CALL THE BALL

An excellent game for children of any age—helps improve catching skills.

What You Need

- A ball that bounces well
- A high brick wall and a paved area to play on
- Several players

What To Do

This is a good game to play with a group of 6–10 children. Give each of the children a number. Then the first child throws the ball up against the wall, calling out a number (make sure they call one of the other children's numbers and not just any number).

Then the child whose number has been called must run forward and catch the ball as it bounces off the wall. If they manage to do this successfully, then they are the next caller. However, if they miss the ball, the first child throws and calls again.

A great party game, played against the wall of the house!

FRENCH CRICKET

A great family game that helps younger children learn some of the skills needed for playing conventional cricket later.

What You Need

- A large soft plastic ball • A small cricket bat, old tennis racquet or piece of wood shaped like a bat

What To Do

Gather the family together to play a fast and furious game of French Cricket. One player holds the bat in front of their legs and the other players space themselves out in a large circle around that player. The object of the game is to try to hit the batsman's legs with the ball.

The batsman has to try to hit the ball away and is not allowed to move except when the ball has been hit and a player is running to fetch it. The batsman can then jump to another position. However, if the player fetching the ball sees their move, the batsman is out.

A fun family game!

335

PUNCH BAG

Next time your children are squabbling, make a punching bag with them so they can punch that instead of each other!

What You Need

- Sugar bag (or sew a calico bag) • Rope
- Filling such as newspaper, old rags, foam, dried grass

What To Do

Your children can fill the bag with the selected filling. Tie a rope securely around the top of the bag and hang it from a beam or the branch of a tree.

A pair of boxing gloves would make a good birthday or Christmas gift to go with the punching bag.

Have a go yourself next time the children have stressed you out! It's better to punch the bag instead of yelling at them.

QUEENIE

Here is another good game for developing your children's catching skills. This one has been around for years.

What You Need

- A medium-sized bouncy ball

What To Do

One child is chosen to be 'Queenie' and stands with their back to the others, who line up a short distance behind that child. 'Queenie' then throws the ball backwards over their head—without looking—and the other children must try to catch it.

When one of the children has caught the ball, they all stand with their hands behind their backs. Then 'Queenie' must turn around and try to guess who has the ball. If they are right, they have a turn at throwing again. If they are wrong, the player with the ball becomes 'Queenie'.

Children really love the part of this game where they hide the ball. No wonder it's been popular for so many years!

SOCK BALL

Make a simple sock ball for the children to have lots of fun with outside.

What You Need

- Tennis ball • A long sock—one of Dad's football or walk socks is ideal

What To Do

Put the tennis ball in the toe of the sock and tie a knot at the other end.

Your children will have lots of fun swinging it, throwing it, bouncing it against walls and catching it.

As my son says, 'They'll have a ball with this game!'

VOLLEYBALL

Young children need lots of fun games with balls to develop ball skills for more formal ball games, such as basketball and netball.

What You Need

• A large soft plastic ball or balloon • A net or rope

What To Do

String up a net or simply a rope from between two trees at just above your child's head height. Bat and throw the ball back and forward to your child. Whoever fails to catch the ball must give a point to the other player.

This game is lots of fun played indoors also, but with a balloon instead of a ball. Simply clear space in a room and tie a string between the backs of two chairs. If you have more players add a few more balloons to increase the fun—and the challenge!

BODY VOLLEYBALL

This game is a variation on traditional volleyball, which is also a good game for the backyard. This is just a little trickier and players will have lots of laughs!

What You Need

• A rope or a net • A soft ball or a balloon • A few players

What To Do

Tie the rope or the net between two trees or posts in the backyard. If you don't have the space, take the children to a local park.

The players divide into two teams on either side of the net. The aim of the game is to toss the ball across the net, not letting it touch the ground. If the ball touches the ground the other team gets a point and the game starts again. The trick with this version is that they can't use their hands. They can use any other part of their bodies—heads, feet, knees, elbows, shoulders and so on—but if anyone uses their hands the other team gets a point.

It is a very funny game and great to play with a balloon also.

FRISBEE FUN

*Frisbees are great for throwing and catching. Take one
to the beach or to a park to throw with the children.*

What You Need

- A frisbee

What To Do

Frisbees are very cheap to buy at toyshops or chain stores. However, you can also use round plastic ice-cream container lids or used disposable plastic plates as frisbees.

Children need help to develop the action required for successful frisbee throwing. Show the children how to hold it horizontally and then swing with their throwing arm, from the chest away from the body. They then let go of the frisbee when the arm is fully extended. With this technique the frisbee floats through the air and is easy to catch.

Have a frisbee throwing contest to see who can throw the longest distance. Play 'catch the frisbee' and keep count of who has caught it the most times.

Frisbees are lots of fun to play with in the water too! Use them in the pool or at the beach.

GOLF BALL TOSS

A fun throwing game that all the family will enjoy playing in the backyard.

What You Need

- Golf balls • Containers such as plastic washing-up dishes, large bowls, buckets, cardboard boxes, ice-cream containers etc. • Ropes or hoops • Cardboard and pencils

What To Do

Arrange a throwing golf course around the backyard. Put out the containers and place a hoop or rope in front of each one so the players are all throwing from the same distance.

The players each have a golf ball and progress around the course trying to 'hole' each container in the least number of throws. Give each player a card so they can keep their own score.

If adults or older siblings are playing younger children, keep it fairer by using a handicap system.

PIGGY IN THE CIRCLE

6+

A group game variation on the old throwing game 'Pig in the Middle'.

What You Need
- A few children • A ball

What To Do

Have the children join hands to form a circle and then drop their hands. One child is chosen to be in the middle of the circle and they are the 'pig'.

The children throw or pass the ball back and forth and the 'pig' tries to catch it. When they do catch the ball, the child who threw it comes into the circle and becomes the new 'pig'.

You can use any size soft ball for this game depending on the throwing and catching skills of the children.

PIGGY IN THE MIDDLE

This is a game that most of us played as children, but have perhaps forgotten.

What You Need

- 3 players • A ball to throw—younger children will cope better with a large, soft ball—the older ones can throw and catch a tennis ball

What To Do

The players stand apart; again this depends on age and throwing and catching ability. The third player is the 'pig' and stands in the middle. The aim of the game is for the two outside players to throw, roll or bounce the ball back and forth to each other without the 'pig' catching it.

If the 'pig' does catch the ball they become one of the outside players and the last thrower goes into the middle as the 'piggy'.

PING PONG BALL CATCH

6+

Make this fun game for the children to use in the back yard,
to increase their hand-eye coordination skills.

What You Need

- An empty plastic 2 litre milk bottle • Thin elastic
- Ping pong ball • Craft knife or sharp kitchen knife

What To Do

Carefully cut off the bottom of the milk bottle with a craft knife or a sharp kitchen knife. Punch a hole near the cut edge on the opposite side to the handle.

Poke a small hole in a ping pong ball and make a knot at one end of the elastic. Force the knot into the hole in the ping pong ball and then cut the elastic to $1/2$–$3/4$ m (2–3 ft). Tie the other end of the elastic to the hole in the bottle and the ball catcher is finished.

The children hold the scoop by the handle, toss the ping pong ball out and try to catch it.

Have a go! It's not as easy as it seems. Have a family competition to see who can catch the ball the most times in a designated period.

Hint!

Cut the bottoms out of plastic milk bottles to use as scoops in the sand pit or in the bath, or wading pool. Leave the lid on though, so the sand or water doesn't escape.

POTATO RACES

This is similar to Egg and Spoon Races for the younger children but a little more challenging!

What You Need

- Metal teaspoons • Potatoes
- Starting and finishing lines

What To Do

Give each competitor a metal teaspoon with a potato placed on it (plastic teaspoons are not strong enough to hold the potatoes). Line them up and on the word 'go', they set off as fast as they can for the finishing line.

However, if they drop their potato, they must scoop it up again with the teaspoon without using their hands, before they continue the race.

Again, slow and steady is often the way to go, as the more intrepid racers usually manage to drop their potatoes.

Give the adults a turn too; it's not as easy as it sounds.

Finish with a sausage sizzle and lots of mash with the bangers, to use up all the bruised spuds.

UNDER AND OVER BALL

6+

A great party game for large groups of children.

What You Need

- Two larger balls, such as basketballs • A whistle

What To Do

Divide the children into two teams and have them line up behind each other in the back yard. You need to have an equal number of children on each team, so if you have an odd number perhaps one child can be the referee and blow the whistle to start the game. Alternatively, join in yourself!

The child at the head of each line has a ball. When the whistle is blown, that child must pass the ball between their legs to the player behind them. Then that child must pass the ball over their head to player behind them, then under, then over and so on. When the last player is reached, that child takes the ball and runs to the head of the line. When the child is at the head of the line, all players on that team sit down, signalling that they have finished and are the winners!

If you have two small teams of children, you can vary the game so that the ball must be passed along the line twice before the game ends. If you have lots of children, you can have more lines and more balls.

This is a great game for teaching teamwork.

ANIMAL, VEGETABLE OR MINERAL BALL

This is a fun party or group game to develop children's throwing and catching skills. It will also make them think!

What You Need

- A few children • A soft ball

What To Do

The children join hands to form a circle and then drop their hands.

They start by throwing the ball at random across the circle. When a child throws the ball they call out either animal, vegetable or mineral and then counts quickly to ten. The catcher must name something from that category before the thrower reaches ten, as well as catching the ball. If they can't or drop the ball they are out. The winner is the last child left in the game.

You can use any sized soft ball for this game, depending on the throwing and catching skills of the children.

BRANDY

A fun, fast and furious game to keep the kids busy in the back yard or a pool.

What You Need

- Children • A soft ball

What To Do

One player is chosen to be 'it' and gives the others a head-start to get away. Then they simply try to hit the others with the ball, but no heads shots are allowed. As soon as someone is hit with the ball they are 'it' and the game continues until all the participants are totally exhausted.

My son assures me it is even more fun to play in a confined area. In a pool, head-shots are allowed as this is all they see, but it would need to be closely supervised by adults. We recently had a holiday in a lovely complex with a large wading pool and this game was very popular with the small fry in the shallow pool.

CAPTAIN BALL

This is another great game to play with a group of children.

What You Need

- Medium-sized soft balls • Lots of children • Space to play

What To Do

Divide the children into teams depending on how many children you have.

The children line up one behind the other, with a leader about three metres in front.

When you say 'go', the leader throws the ball to each member of the team in turn, who throws it back and then bobs down.

When the last person in the team receives the ball, they call 'up' and run to the throwing position.

The old leader runs to the front of the team and it starts all over again.

The game is finished when the team is back to where it began, with the original leader in the front throwing position.

DONKEY

Most adults will remember this game from their own childhood.
Play it again with your children and their friends.

What You Need

- Children • A tennis ball

What To Do

This was one of my favourite playground games at primary school and the children of today will enjoy it, too.

The children line up facing a wall—about two metres from it—except for the person who is 'it'. This person is the ball thrower; all the players will have a turn at this. The player with the ball throws the ball at the wall and, as it rebounds, everyone must jump over it. If a player is hit or touched by the ball they gain a letter, eventually spelling D O N K E Y! The player is out when they get the whole word.

The winner of each game is the person who has the least number of letters when the game ends. Time each game so everyone can have a turn at throwing and keep a score sheet to see who is the overall winner.

FITNESS STATIONS

Stop the kids turning into couch potatoes by setting up some fitness stations in the back yard.

What You Need

• Hoops, ropes, witches hats and so on • Skipping ropes

What To Do

Set up a few fitness stations in the backyard. The stations will depend on what equipment you have.

Mark out the first with a rope or the garden hose and the kids can do 10 star jumps. Then if you have a trampoline they can run over and do 15 jumps.

Mark out the next station with some toys or witches hats and they have to do 10 push ups. Next they run over to the skipping ropes and, using a bottle timer, they skip until it's emptied or they have done one hundred skips.

The winner gets to decide on the stations for the next race. Look out when they challenge Mum or Dad to a go!

PLAYING ORGANISED SPORT

Encourage your children to join a sporting club or team if they are interested.

What You Need

- Time

What To Do

Children need to have outlets for their physical energy and, while sporting team time can eat into family outing time, it is still great to encourage children to join and take an interest in sport.

Lifetime hobbies and interests are often begun in childhood. Many adults are still playing sports such as bowls, golf, tennis etc. into their eighties and are healthier and more alert for it.

It may mean that, as parents, we drive our children to practices and spend precious weekend time watching soccer, footy or netball games, but the physical and interpersonal skills our children develop by being part of a team make up for the commitment we put in.

I believe it is important for the years ahead that children learn to lose and win gracefully, to work as a team and to accept the knocks that sport can give. Just remember, however, that it still needs to be fun for them and we mustn't push our own agendas as parents.

PRACTICE WALL TENNIS

If your children are keen to learn tennis this is an excellent way to begin.

What You Need

• Tennis balls • Tennis racquets • A practice wall

What To Do

Children's tennis rackets are not very expensive and make a great gift. Grandparents are often glad to have practical suggestions for Christmas and birthday presents. Adult racquets are not suitable for young children as they are too big, too heavy, and the grips are too large for their smaller hands.

Most tennis courts have a practice wall where you can take children to have a hit together free of charge. Many schools allow public access to their courts on weekends and after school and, if they have tennis or multi-purpose courts, they usually have practice walls also.

It takes a long time for children to be consistent enough to hit the ball to themselves on a practice wall but you can hit it to them, taking it in turn to hit the ball.

As their skills improve, introduce some of the other shots such as volleys and smashes. If they are really interested and show some skill, think about tennis lessons. Most towns and cities have well-organised Junior Tennis Associations where kids can play in junior competitions, have a lot of fun and make lots of new friends.

TENNIS ON A POLE

Make this simple game for the children to play in the backyard and help develop the good hand-eye co-ordination that is so essential for many sports.

What You Need

- A broom handle • A metal swivel
- Elastic joined to a tennis ball (available from sports stores)
- Two plastic racquets

What To Do

Hammer or screw the swivel to the top of the broom stick. Attach the elastic to the swivel and tie so the ball reaches half-way down the broom stick. Dig a hole in the garden for the broom stick making sure there is plenty of room around it for the ball to swing and for the children to play.

The children take it in turn to hit the ball and make it swing around the stick. Use only small bats or small plastic tennis racquets if two children are playing. If one child is playing on his own they could use a junior tennis racquet safely.

You may like to play with the children. It is lots of fun, good exercise and harder than it sounds!

THROW AND KNEEL

A fast and furious throwing game to play with a group of children.

What You Need

- A large soft ball • Children

What To Do

The children join hands to make a circle and then drop hands. One child or an adult stands in the middle to be the thrower. The children have to concentrate because the thrower can throw the ball to anyone—first he calls their name and then quickly throws it.

If a child misses a ball they have to go into a half kneeling position, with one knee down and one knee up. If they catch the ball on their next turn they can stand up again. If they miss again they then have to go into a full kneel with both knees down. Then if they catch the ball they go into a half kneel, and the next time they catch it they can stand. If they miss a third time in a row they are out of the game.

The game continues until only one person if left and a new thrower is nominated. This game should be played fast and it is a lot of fun, as well as being great throwing and catching practice.

BASKETBALL RECORDS

Challenge the kids to a basketball competition to see who is champ.

What You Need

- Basketball • Basketball hoop

What To Do

If you don't have a basketball hoop at home take the children to a park where there is one. See who can shoot the most baskets in a row without missing one. Keep count and at the end of the day see who has the record for the most baskets shot in a row.

Keep the record on the fridge or noticeboard and, next time the children challenge you, see who can beat the family record.

BOUNCE WITH A PARTNER

When your children are really competent ball bouncers, increase the challenge by using two balls and bouncing with a friend, sibling, Mum or Dad.

What You Need

- Two tennis balls or other small bouncy balls
- A flat area to bounce balls outdoors

What To Do

This is much trickier than simply bouncing balls on your own. The two players stand 1¹/₂ m (5 ft) apart and increase the distance between them as they go through the routine. The idea is to throw and catch using the two balls at the same time.

Bounce the ball to your child and catch with both hands
Bounce the ball to your child and catch in your right hand with the palm up
Bounce the ball to your child and catch in your left hand with the palm up
Bounce the ball to your child and catch in your right hand with the palm down
Bounce the ball to your child and catch in your left hand with the palm down
Bounce the ball to your child and clap before you catch

Discard one ball and practice bouncing the ball to your child, who bounces it back without catching it. See how many times you can do this without stopping.

Now try to do it and clap once before you receive the ball. Think of other skills you can try together.

ELASTICS

My primary school friends and I spent most lunch hours playing elastics! If you remember how, teach it to your own children.

What You Need

- 2–3 m (6–9 ft) of elastic knotted to make a big loop • 3 children

What To Do

This game needs three players (although I can remember that my sister and I used to play it at home with a chair at one end).

Players take it in turn to be the jumper; the others stand inside the elastic and move apart until the elastic is taut. The elastic goes around their ankles with their feet about a shoulder-width apart. The jumper starts outside the elastic and then:

Jumps in

Jumps out again with a leg on either side of the elastic

Jumps inside again

Jumps onto both strands of elastic

Jumps onto one strand with both feet

Jumps out to one side with both feet under a strand and then jumps over to the other side taking that strand with their feet

Jumps out so the elastic goes back into place

Then the whole sequence is repeated from the other side. A player is out when they make a mistake in a sequence or they can't manage one of the moves. They then become one of the supports at one end of the elastic and one of those children has the next turn.

Encourage children to think of other variations to the routine.

ELASTICS CHALLENGE

When the children have mastered the basic moves of the
game of elastics see if they can perform these moves.

What You Need

- 2–3 m (6–9 ft) of elastic knotted to make a big loop
  - 3 children

What To Do

To increase the challenge, elastics can be played with the elastic around the holders' knees so the player jumping has to jump higher.

The children may also like to try these moves:

Jump in while the holders have their feet close together so the elastic is narrower

Jump in but the elastic is at knee level

Jump onto one strand with both feet with the elastic at knee level

Jump out—to one side with both feet under a strand and then jumps over to the other side taking that strand with their feet—this is done with the elastic at hip level

If they really master this game they can try jumping with the elastic at waist level. Have a turn yourself and see if you can still remember some of those old playground tricks!

PADDLING

Paddling is a skill that takes some time to acquire but develops great arm, shoulder and chest muscles.

What You Need

- Surf ski, canoe or kayak

What To Do

For a while I lived on a canal on the Gold Coast and paddled my surf ski most days for fun and exercise. I became extremely fit in quite a short time. Teach these paddling skills to your children. If you don't have a canoe, surf ski or kayak, hire one occasionally.

If you live close to still water such as a lake that you can use for recreational purposes, think about buying one to use with the family.

Warning!

Make sure the children wear a life jacket when paddling a canoe, surf ski or kayak.

SEVENSES

This was one of our favourite games at primary school. Your children will love playing it if you have a wall to bounce against at home.

What You Need

- Players • A tennis or other soft, small, bouncy ball

What To Do

The players take it in turns—when a player drops the ball the next person has a turn. There are many ways to play this game but the one I remember went like this:

7 times	throw the ball against the wall and catch it with two hands
6 times	throw the ball against the wall and catch it with one hand
5 times	throw the ball against the wall, let it bounce and catch it
4 times	throw the ball under your leg against the wall then catch it
3 times	throw the ball, clap your hands once and catch it
2 times	throw the ball, turn around, let it bounce and catch it
Once	throw the ball, let it bounce, bounce it with your hand, and catch it

When you have another turn, you start at the turn where you dropped the ball rather than have to begin all over again.

TUNNEL BALL

*Tunnel ball is great fun for children and, as well as teaching them
ball skills, helps them develop socially as they work in a team.*

What You Need

• Lots of children • Two large round balls • Room to play

What To Do

Divide the children into two teams and line them up one behind the other. The children stand with
their legs apart forming as straight a tunnel as possible. The child at the end of each team
crouches down ready to receive the ball.

When you say 'go' the child at the top of each team tunnels the ball as fast and as accurately
through the tunnel as they can to the child at the end.

That player runs to the top of the team and it is then their turn to tunnel the ball through. Remind
the children before they begin to make sure they remember to crouch down when they are at the
end of the team. I have seen many a ball go rolling over the oval on sports day because someone
forgot to catch it. The players also have to be ready to reach down to push the ball through the
tunnel and to retrieve it as quickly as possible if it goes out of the tunnel.

When every player has had a turn at tunnelling and the original leader is back at the front that
team is the winner!

ZAP

A fast and furious game to play with a group of children.

What You Need

- A tennis ball • Some children

What To Do

Choose one of the children to be the first zapper. This child chases the other children and tries to hit them with the ball below the shoulder. When a player is hit they join the first zapper and they both try to hit the other players. The game continues until only one player is left and they become the new zapper.

In summer this game is fun to play with a wet ball or even with a large supply of water bombs.

SPECIAL
OCCASIONS

CHRISTMAS PASTA DECORATIONS

Pasta glued onto cardboard makes cheap, but decorative, Christmas decorations. Make some with your children this Christmas.

What You Need

- Pasta of different shapes and sizes • Cardboard
- Can of gold spray paint • String or gold ribbon
- PVA Glue

What To Do

Cut the cardboard into small shapes—circles, rectangles and squares—with your children. Then punch a hole in each to tie it on the Christmas tree. Then help the children glue an assortment of different pasta shapes onto the cardboard. They look great glued on both sides, so wait until one side is completely dry and then they can glue some on the other side.

When they have made enough, take them outside and carefully spray them with the gold spray paint (definitely an adult job).

When the paint has dried, thread some gold ribbon or Christmas tie through the holes and hang them on the tree. Wait for the compliments!

CHRISTMAS SCENTED PINE CONES

5+

Make some attractive scented pine cones together to decorate your home at Christmas. Or give some away as special gifts!

What You Need

- Pine cones • Scissors • Cloves • Red or green ribbon
- Red or green crepe • Thumb tacks or craft glue
- Paper or fabric

What To Do

Show your children how to wrap each clove in a tiny piece of the crepe paper or fabric and insert into the pine cones (do this part carefully because some pine cones are quite prickly). When all the holes are filled, help them attach a length of red, green or 'Christmassy' ribbon to hang it by. The ribbon can be glued to the top of the pine cone with strong craft glue, or attached with a tack.

These decorations look lovely hanging from the tree, or hang several with different length ribbons together from a curtain track.

CHRISTMAS SNOWFLAKES

*Use up scraps of gold, silver and Christmas paper by making
pretty Christmas snowflakes with your children.*

What You Need

- Coloured paper • Scissors
- Ribbon • Blu-Tack

What To Do

Help your children cut up the scraps of paper into different sized squares. Next, they fold the paper square into a triangle and then fold it again. They then cut out notches along the edges with their scissors. When they open out the paper they will have beautiful snowflakes.

Hang them with a coloured wrapping ribbon and attach them to the ceiling with small blobs of Blu-Tack. They will look pretty and festive hanging above your Christmas tree, or twirling in front of an open window.

EASTER EGGS

Eggs are traditionally associated with our Easter celebrations. Decorate some eggs with your children and serve coloured boiled eggs for breakfast on Easter Sunday.

What You Need

- Eggs • Birthday cake candles
- Food dyes • Masking tape

What To Do

Make up strong solutions of red, yellow and blue food dyes (white eggs dye best so try and find a dozen at a supermarket with lots of white eggs).

Boil the eggs for at least ten minutes. Hard boiled eggs are best to use with younger children and will last as decorations for the Easter period out of the fridge (unless you live in the tropics). However, with older children you can use blown eggs which of course, while more fragile to work with, will last much longer.

To blow eggs use a large tapestry or darning needle and make holes at both ends—larger at one end then the other. Use the needle to carefully pierce the yolk sac a few times. Blow from the smaller hole end, making sure you get all the egg out of the shell or later the egg will smell. Save the egg for scrambled eggs, omelette or other cooking. Blown eggs must be decorated before blowing.

To decorate, give your children a thin birthday cake candle to draw interesting designs on the eggs. If you want to have multicoloured eggs, wrap sections of the egg with masking tape. Then use a spoon to dip the egg in the food dyes. Remove the masking tape gradually and you will end up with multi-coloured decorated eggs.

6+

CHRISTMAS WRAPPING PAPER

Save money and have fun too by making your own individual Christmas wrapping paper with your children.

What You Need

- Red and green paint (acrylic paint works best and is available from toy or art and craft shops)
- Two kitchen sponges • Two plastic plates or polystyrene trays • Potatoes • Sharp knife
- Glitter • Newsprint paper

What To Do

Place the kitchen sponges on the plates and pour a little green paint on one and red on the other. Spread the paint thickly across the sponges.

Next, cut some large potatoes in half and carefully cut some simple Christmas shapes out of them with a sharp knife. The shapes must stick out at least 2 cm ($^3/_4$ in) above the rest of the potato half. Stars, bells, Christmas trees or a candy cane all look effective.

Your children press the potato onto the paint then print with it on the newsprint. While the paint is still wet, sprinkle a little gold or silver glitter on to add a festive touch.

Your Christmas gifts will look wonderful wrapped in your children's art work.

NEW YEAR RESOLUTIONS

6+

Teach your children some traditions to see in the New Year and encourage them to being something new—maybe keep their room tidier or pick up their toys without being nagged by Mum or Dad!

What You Need

- Time together

What To Do

Do some reading about New Year traditions and discuss them with your children. The Scots celebrate New Year in a big way with their Hogmanay festival and the Chinese New Year (which occurs later in January to mid-February) is a great festival to be part of. If you have a Chinatown near where you live, there is usually a procession. Or you could take your children to a Chinese restaurant for lunch to sample some yummy Yum Cha.

Together plan some New Year resolutions and make a list. Involve the rest of the family too! Check your lists again in March and see how everyone is going. Perhaps you could make some family resolutions too, like making Sundays a family day where you try to do something special together.

SAINT PATRICK'S DAY

Celebrate the 17th March, St. Patrick's Day, with your children.

What You Need

- Irish songs • Irish stories • Green food

What To Do

Explain to your children who St. Patrick was. Many families have links with Ireland. If yours does, see if you have any photos you can look at together of your Irish ancestors. Find Ireland in the atlas or go to the library and borrow some books about Ireland.

Finally, cook some Irish stew for tea with your children and serve it with green mashed potatoes and green cordial!

SHROVE TUESDAY PANCAKES

Shrove Tuesday is the Tuesday just before Lent begins. Lent is the period of forty days before Easter and is a time of fasting. Make some pancakes together with your children for breakfast or dessert on Shrove Tuesday (Pancake Tuesday).

What You Need

- Kitchen utensils • 1 cup sifted plain flour
- 1 egg • 1 cup milk • Pinch salt • Butter for cooking

What To Do

Your children can help you collect the ingredients. Beat the egg and stir in the flour and salt. Gradually add the milk to the mixture and stir until it is smooth.

I prefer to make pancakes in a jug as it is easier to pour the mixture into a pan. Melt a small amount of butter in the crepe pan and pour in enough mixture to cover the base of the pan. Turn once.

We love pancakes with lemon juice and castor sugar or strawberries in our family. You will probably have your own favourite topping.

ANZAC DAY

*Many children come home puzzled and concerned because of talk
about war at school before Anzac Day or Remembrance Day.
Use this opportunity to talk to them about past wars.*

What You Need

- Time

What To Do

Explain to your children the history of the World Wars, perhaps using an atlas to show where the distant countries are in the world.

Explain the significance of the word Anzac (Australian and New Zealand Army Corps) and about Gallipoli. Tell them why veterans still march on Anzac Day and the meaning of Remembrance Day (the first World War finished in 1918 on the 11th hour of the 11th day of the 11th month).

Perhaps some older relations have some medals or other war memorabilia to look at or old photos. Take your children to an Anzac parade or a dawn wreath laying ceremony.

Older children may enjoy watching a video such as 'Gallipoli' with you.

CHRISTMAS NEWSPAPER

A great way to keep in touch with distant family and friends at Christmas time.

What You Need

• Family photos • Family news • Pencils • Paper

What To Do

Suggest to your children a few weeks before Christmas that they could help you make a family newspaper to be sent to family and friends with the Christmas cards.

They can be the 'reporters' gathering news and interesting items from the rest of the family. They might like to try their hand at drawing some cartoons or pictures to include in it.

If you have a computer and printer, printing the newspaper will be simple. If not, collate it and take it to your nearest photocopying shop.

Lots of fun and the folks you send it to will love receiving it.

7+

CHRISTMAS TREE ORNAMENTS

Mix up a batch of baker's clay and make some very individual decorations for your Christmas tree.

What You Need

- 3 cups plain flour • 1 cup salt • 1 teaspoon glycerine (buy it from a pharmacy—it is also useful for adding to bubble mixture to make bubbles stronger) • 1 cup water • Mixing bowl
- Christmas shaped biscuit or play dough cutters
- Thick nail, skewer or knitting needle

What To Do

Mix the flour and salt and add the glycerine. Pour in the water, stirring as you add it. Mix until the mixture is fairly stiff and the children will enjoy kneading it until it is smooth like bread. The children can roll out the dough until it is a couple of centimetres thick.

Set them up on a table outside with plastic or vinyl cloth and the cutters, and they will have great fun making shapes. Show them how to make a hole near the top of each shape with the nail so they can hang the decoration.

Put the shapes on a baking tray and bake slowly in a cool oven until they are hard. When the dough is dried, the children will have fun painting their decorations with Christmas colours. Provide some glitter to sprinkle on while the paint is wet.

When they have dried the children can thread some thin Christmas ribbon or wrapping ribbon through the holes and hang them on the tree.

EASTER EGG CLUES

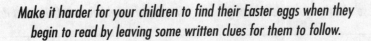

Make it harder for your children to find their Easter eggs when they begin to read by leaving some written clues for them to follow.

What You Need

- Paper • Pen • Easter Eggs

What To Do

Begin the clues at the bottom of their bed, in the basket they've left out for their eggs or wherever else the Easter Bunny usually leaves the eggs in at your place. Be as creative as you can in thinking of clues such as:

Look in the place where the dirty socks go (the dirty washing basket)

Under the tree where the lemons grow

Look beside where you like to swing

Make the clues simple enough for emergent readers to sound out, or use words they already know. Eventually they will find the treasure trove of eggs but hopefully they will have used up a little energy and practised their reading before they get there.

CHRISTMAS STARS

These biscuits make delightful gifts for friends and neighbours at Christmas time.

What You Need

- 1¼ cups plain flour • 90 g (3 oz) softened butter
- 1 tablespoon white vinegar • 1 tablespoon water
- Strawberry or raspberry jam • Beaten egg for glazing

What To Do

Using a large bowl, rub the butter into the flour with fingertips until it resembles fine crumbs. Mix the vinegar with the water and add to the mixture, to form a firm dough.

Lightly knead on a floured board until it is smooth. Wrap it in some plastic food wrap and chill in the fridge for about an hour. On a lightly floured board roll out the dough until it is about 5 mm (¼ in) thick.

Cut it into 6 cm (2 ½ in) squares. Then, using a small knife, cut from the corner of each square to almost the centre. Next, carefully fold the right hand corner of each section in to meet at the centre. Press firmly so they stay down.

Put a little jam in the centre of each star and glaze the stars with lightly beaten egg white, using a brush. Bake on an ungreased baking tray for 10 minutes in a moderate oven. Cool on biscuit racks and store in airtight containers until needed.

Hint!

Christmas stars look lovely wrapped in red or green cellophane and tied with red, gold and green curling ribbon.

CHRISTMAS WREATH

Older children will love making a colourful Christmas wreath.

What You Need

- Glue gun • Twig wreath base • Selection of dried leaves, flowers, pine cones, wheat
- Gold or silver spray paint • Christmas tartan ribbon • Wide red ribbon

What To Do

Visit your local flower markets with the children and buy any of the bits and pieces you need that you can't collect from your own garden or local parks.

Set the children up outdoors, with newspaper spread out to protect tables and pavers. Decide which items they would like to spray and do this first on plenty of paper away from furniture. Leave to dry.

You will have to help with the gluing as glue guns can give a nasty burn. Attach a string loop to the top of the wreath for hanging. Next, help the children tie lots of small bows with the tartan ribbon to be interspaced on the wreath. They will enjoy deciding where to position all the other bits and pieces and helping you glue them in place on the twig wreath.

Leave a space at the bottom for a large bow and attach this last of all. Hang it on the front door for a lovely Christmassy entrance to your home.

COLOURFUL PASTA WREATHS

This idea came from Karen Bourne, another teacher here on the Gold Coast and the wife of my son's soccer coach. Thanks, Karen!

What You Need

- Paper plates • Dried pasta of various shapes and sizes
- PVA glue • Gold or silver spray paint • Christmas ribbon
- Hole punch

What To Do

This is easy enough for older children to do on their own. It is best done outside—especially the painting.

Begin by cutting the middle out of the paper plates, leaving the crinkly edge. Next, use the hole punch to punch a hole in one spot; this will be the top of the wreath. Then use the strong glue to stick pasta all over the remaining plate until it is well covered.

When the glue is completely dry, your children will need to put down lots of newspaper before they spray their wreaths really well (don't spray on windy days and make sure they follow the directions on the spray can carefully).

When the paint is completely dry the children can tie a lovely tartan or Christmas ribbon to the bottom of their unusual wreath.

Perhaps they could make some to sell to friends, family or the neighbours for Christmas funds or make some to give as gifts. These would also be great at school fetes.

EASTER CANDLE CARVING

A simple, but most effective decoration for your children to make for Easter.

What You Need

- White wax candles • Small knife
- Sharp pencil • Acrylic paint • Rags

What To Do

Your children warm a candle by rubbing it between their hands. Next, they carefully scratch a pattern onto the candle with the pencil and, using the knife, they carve out the pattern (be sure to have close adult supervision when the children are using the knife).

When they have finished, they polish the candle with a soft rag and then rub the candle surface with some acrylic paint, making sure the paint goes into the carved surface.

When the paint is dry they polish it again with a soft cloth.

Group the candles together for a decorative effect and light them for Easter lunch.

ACTIVITY INDEX